Developing the Observing Eye

Teacher Observation and Assessment in Early Childhood Education

DEVELOPING THE OBSERVING EYE

TEACHER OBSERVATION AND ASSESSMENT
IN
EARLY CHILDHOOD EDUCATION

BY

CYNTHIA MURPHY-LANG

Behold the Child with Reverence,
Teach the Child with Love,
And let the Child go forth in Freedom.
                                    – Rudolf Steiner

Printed with support from the Waldorf Curriculum Fund

Published by:
Waldorf Publications at the
Research Institute for Waldorf Education
38 Main Street
Chatham, NY 12037

Title: *Developing the Observing Eye: Teacher Observation and Assessment in Early Childhood Education*
Author: Cynthia Murphy-Lang
Editor: David Mitchell
Copy Editor and Proofreader: Ann Erwin
Cover Design: David Mitchell
Photographs: Courtesy of Zoe Adlersberg, the New Amsterdam Early Childhood Center, and the Garden City Waldorf School
– rights secured by author
ISBN # 978-1-888365-96-2

Original printing by McNaughton & Gunn
Saline, MI 48176 USA
February 2010

Reprinted by CreateSpace
June 2014

TABLE OF CONTENTS

Observation and Assessment

FOREWORD

There are occasions when we look at something, perhaps an x-ray of our own arm, or we listen to something, perhaps our raspy breathing, and we wonder what it means. We are aware that to the diagnosing doctor these indicators mean so much more. Albert Szent-Georgi, a twice-awarded Nobel prize winner, described this phenomenon well when he said, "Discovery is seeing what everyone else is seeing but thinking what no one else has thought."

This book is an invitation to discover what a highly skilled Waldorf preschool and kindergarten teacher is thinking when he or she sees. Cynthia Lang brings stunning clarity to the components of human development as indicated by Rudolf Steiner. These components lay the groundwork for the art and science of the Waldorf approach to child observation.

She then moves on in a seamless fashion to prepare the reader/ teacher for the first encounters with the child, the parent, and the classroom. The Waldorf teacher, already familiar with working through sleep and dreams to organize the experiences of the day, will find this section truly inspiring as Ms. Lang guides the teacher through the key encounters and reflections on those encounters.

Finally, Ms. Lang broaches a very sensitive topic for the Waldorf teacher: the possibility of structured observation that can serve to document the readiness of a child for transitions from preschool to kindergarten and from kindergarten to first grade. In the Waldorf approach to education this advancement to the next level is not a foregone conclusion, but a matter of readiness. However, if this critical, subjective decision is made by the teacher without proper involvement of the parents and clear documentation, it can be very upsetting to some parents. Ms. Lang offers a true gift to the Movement in this final section, as she presents structured assessment forms and clear explanations of their use.

For the reader coming to the work of Rudolf Steiner for the first time, and more familiar with the educational processes of the public schools, this book offers a very different but equally fascinating experience. The reader will find the writing to be richly poetic. It can be experienced as a journey of discovery and insight, but a journey that begins with a very steep climb. The first section discusses the key variables of human development as Steiner presented them. To the uninitiated, this is clearly the most challenging portion of the book. The paradigms are so different from traditional science that they simply need to be held for the reader as possibilities in the beginning. As the book unfolds, they make progressively more sense, and their usefulness for organizing perception is revealed.

The second section, a Waldorf view of the significance of beginning school, a home visit, meeting the parents, preparing the classroom and greeting the child, is very likely to set up a deep longing in the reader. It can generate a wish that they had been held in such a way, and a desire to encourage all teachers to move in this tender and profoundly caring direction.

Finally, the third section will seem like a fascinating proposal — to consider the possibility that assessment can be done with structure and refined attention, but without the need for quantifiable testing. As schools struggle with the burden of incessant evaluations and accountability procedures that seem to cast doubt on the teacher's natural ability to meet the children and teach them, this section reads like a breath of fresh air.

There is much that can be harvested from this book and adapted to general use. May both groups of readers be inspired in their own ways as they enjoy this fine contribution to educational literature.

— Dee Joy Coulter, Ed.D.

Introduction

The purpose of this book is to explore and develop a process of educational assessment in the early childhood years for children being educated in Waldorf schools. If we can observe how the young child moves in form, develops, grows, and takes in the world through his developing senses, it is conceivable that we will begin to understand how the child learns.

It is my intent to develop an on-going process, a process that is first of all based in observation, observations that are thoughtfully pondered and explored through the questions they present. It is a process that includes the child, the parent and the teachers, calling forth a community of care that is specific to the present and future needs of the growing and developing human being. It is a process that recognizes the understanding of the human being as described by Rudolf Steiner. Although the focus of this book is early childhood, the understanding Steiner brought to the world is deeply embedded in the Waldorf curriculum and progresses throughout the child's school life into adulthood.

This process does not deny the value or practice of individual assessment; it includes assessment tools. But the understanding of human development, observation and compassionate thinking are the primary requirements of the process. It is not enough to simply formulate a one-time assessment for school readiness or individual need. It is not enough to assume that within a single assessment we can determine who the child is and how the child is living within his form or in the world. A one-time assessment will bind a label to a child and will not necessarily reveal the gifts or hindrances the child faces. An individual assessment alone cannot explore how the child works with his hindrances and gifts. Nor can a single assessment reveal how gifts may develop out of what appears to be a child's hindrance. A human being is not born 'world ready.' A human being takes time to find a place in the world. A human being is a book with many pages, and each new life deserves to be read with reverence, love and in freedom.

To begin, it is important to take a moment to understand a little about Waldorf education and how and why Steiner chose the form he did for transforming educational practices. It is also important to explore what these educational practices demand of those of us who endeavor to take them up.

At the beginning of the twentieth century, socialism was seen as the cure for the class system that dominated in the industrial age. It may be hard to believe, but in the United States there were many children who did not receive an education even a hundred years ago. Education was the right of the upper class and lack of education was assurance that the lower class would continue to exist. Socialism offered the view that all individuals deserved at least an elementary school education. The public school system came into existence and made education the right of all citizens. We do not like to think of education this way, but actually public schools became a means of socializing America's children. Steiner was very aware of the shortfalls of public education and the deepening rift between practical work and spiritual life.

> Our school system is marked especially by features that
> reflect the tendencies toward decline in modern cultural
> life. The social structures of modern governments have not
> followed the requirements of actual life. For instance, they
> have taken on a form that does not satisfy the economic
> demands of modern humanity. They have also set this
> same backward stamp upon the school system, which,
> having liberated it from the religious confessions, they have
> now brought it into complete dependence on themselves.
> At every level, schools mold human beings into the forms
> the state requires for doing what the state deems necessary.
> (Steiner, 1906, p.1)

Rudolf Steiner perceived the importance of education in building a healthy social organism, and with the help of Emil Molt, he founded the first Waldorf school and began to work to bring about changes in all realms of practical and social life. What is really different about Waldorf education? Steiner presented a picture of human development which describes the human being as a four-fold organism that is formed out of the elements of earth (physical body), water (etheric body), air (astral body) and warmth (ego body). He also described the being of man as three-fold: body, soul and spirit, capable of thinking, feeling and willing. He ascribed to the human being a wise, moral and timely development with a destiny and purpose related to the earth. Out of these thoughts and observations Steiner formed a divinely wise curriculum.

> The real need of the present is that the schools be totally grounded in a free spiritual and cultural life. What should be taught and cultivated in these schools must be drawn solely from knowledge of the growing human being and of individual capacities. A genuine anthropology must form the basis of education and instruction. The question should not be: What does a human being need to know and be able to do for the social order that now exists, but rather: What capacities are latent in this human being, and what lies within that can be developed? Then it will be possible to bring ever new forces into the social order from the rising generations. The life of the social order will be what is made of it by a succession of fully developed human beings who take their places in the social order. The rising generation should not be molded into what the existing social order chooses to make of it. (Steiner, 1906, p.2)

Although Steiner lived over a hundred years ago, his thoughts are thoroughly modern and current. The education Steiner proposed is only eighty-five years old, an infant in pedagogical practice.

The greatest question is not if Waldorf education should exist; it is currently the largest independent school movement in the world. The question is how parents, teachers and administrators can join in this task of creating an education that supports the free development of their children and students. What does a community look like that supports a Waldorf school? How do we sort out the massive information coming toward us that is not actually new, but chains us to the old mechanistic view of the human being? How do we overcome long-held opinions that paralyze us in the fear of creating new forms? How do we overcome our inability to enter into community together for the sake of the children's freedom and ultimately our own freedom?

The answer lies in the children who bring us together. If we can learn to keep the children at the center of our thoughts, then perhaps we will begin to ask the questions that may help us to seek transformation in ourselves. These children need us to be worthy of their imitation. How do we do that? We do that by being willing to go out on a limb and seek to know ourselves and transform whatever leads to stagnation, chaos or war. We need to try to work together and not deny one person because of differences, or personal views of social interaction, or any aspect which creates difficulty. We must work against personal power or the desire to be revered. We must work not to seek results, but to love the work itself. "Work undertaken for the sake of results is the least likely to produce them, and learning unaccompanied by reverence is unlikely to advance us far. Love for the work, not for the results, alone moves us forward." (Steiner, 1994, p.104) We must find the enthusiasm to bring the world and all that it offers to the children. We must recognize that young children need us to understand that they are nourished through the senses and must have an appropriate diet as they begin to explore the world. And we must recognize that children have a process of development that is timely and lawful. We must struggle to put all of this together for the sake of the children. Struggle is the beginning of questioning. Struggle is the puzzle that leads to the destiny of the children who are writing their biography before our very eyes. This community for the children can be a wonderful symbiotic microcosm that leads all of us to personal development and transformation and will eventually require social changes in the macrocosmic community.

If parents, teachers and school administrators can see their children as unfolding biographies (each child is a book that we are reading) and that these children are chapters in the unfolding biography of the school and the school is a chapter in the ongoing evolution of the human being and the world that surrounds us, then our shared observations and actions on behalf of the children will form the school community that cares for the children. The actions of all involved in the community must be focused on meaningful work, the work human beings do and not on fixing the child. If our actions are focused on work, then we will build a school community which will reflect a healthy social life. We will be part of a community that creates new forms out of a unique understanding of human development.

Now having explored a little the impulse behind Rudolf Steiner's thinking when he developed Waldorf education, it is time to look at assessment in the early years and the components of human development he introduced.

To Assess or Not to Assess, That Is the Question

In a recent conversation a Waldorf early childhood teacher asked an anthroposophical school doctor if he thought we should be doing first grade readiness assessments in the kindergarten.

Waldorf early childhood teachers make every effort to give children in their care an appropriate environment which allows them to grow freely in the early years. Inclusion and the formation of the class are two of a Waldorf early childhood teacher's primary tasks. Labels and extreme individualization are avoided with determined effort.

There is a belief among many Waldorf early childhood educators that they have a responsibility to protect young children from outside labels, tests, observations and screenings because this is the only way the children can overcome or outgrow their difficulties. Their concern is well founded. The mayor of New York City, Michael Bloomberg, was given the power to take over the public school system. He has made testing and accountability the byword of education in New York City. In return for positive results in test scores, he offers schools and teachers monetary incentives. Until now testing has been focused on school age children third grade and up. In August he sent an email to all public elementary school principals offering to pay for a five-year study, testing children in kindergarten, first and second grades in math and reading through a ninety minute test using pencil and paper or a hand-held palm pad. (Gootman, 8/26/08) Each year the government, through the enactment of No Child Left Behind, a program run not by educators, but by politicians, transforms our schools into warehouses for test takers. Teaching to the test rather than teaching the children has become the rule.

Along with this new standard for education comes earlier and earlier assessments to determine the need for intervention that often end up labeling children permanently. An understanding of children, their readiness to learn and how they learn individually cannot be part of a standardized testing and labeling program. Some children do struggle, even in kindergarten, and the question that arises is this: Is the inability to accept a need for early intervention a blind spot in Waldorf early childhood programs or is it a salvation of the child?

What happens when a child cannot fit into that beautiful and inclusive environment? What happens when the child ruins the circle, the puppet show or all the well-planned elements of a Waldorf early childhood program? What happens when a child presents behaviors such as pinching, hitting, refusing to speak, kicking his boots off in the park, swearing and being disrespectful? What happens when one child takes up all of the teacher's time and attention? What happens when, as rising first graders, they are very far from being ready to work with the first grade curriculum? What happens is the following: The teachers bring their frustrations to their colleagues in faculty meetings and child study or to the parents in a conference. Because there is not a process in place to determine if something is going on besides poor parenting and bad habits, the child is labeled a behavior problem and is sometimes asked to leave the school.

The point I am trying to make is this: Children in Waldorf early childhood programs are being informally assessed, especially children who present behaviors which their teachers cannot cope with in the classroom. When teachers react to behavior it is natural to search for a cause for that behavior. There is a tendency to look for a cause within the environment surrounding the child, usually outside the classroom, since the teacher assumes the environment of the classroom has been carefully thought out. The nature of the young child is predominately imitative, so the behavior must come from someone or some experience within the child's home environment.

However, when we look outside the child exclusively in search of a cause or a place to lay blame, we form opinions. Opinions are based on assumptions, not observable facts. Nevertheless, our opinions become our assessments of the child. "We must always remember that where we have already formed a conclusion we cannot learn anything. If we desire only to judge, we can learn nothing." (Steiner, 1994, p.105) These opinions remain with the children and sometimes cause rejection because we do not understand what the children are telling us with their behaviors. We do not have a process for observation which helps us to gather information about the child that might enlighten and guide us towards a way of working with the children differently. Perhaps even finding a way to support them so that their pain is eased and their hindrances are overcome or transformed into abilities.

A healthy and reasonable assessment of the child using observation and an imaginative process in a protective classroom environment, performed by the child's teacher and perhaps an educational support teacher who has a background in early childhood education, is much more supportive of the child's healthy development. The next question is: What do we need to know?

Perhaps it would be helpful at this point to take a look at how mainstream special educators define educational assessment. An educational assessment process is put in place to determine the presence of a suspected learning disability. The process includes the following parts: collection, analysis, evaluation, determination and recommendation. The first step in an assessment process involves collecting or gathering information from parents, teachers, school or medical records and a review of the child's educational, social, developmental and environmental history. Once this information has been gathered, the next step involves analyzing or thinking about the information to determine a need for evaluation. Evaluation can involve testing of the child's academic, intellectual, psychological, emotional, perceptional, language, cognitive, and medical development in order to determine areas of strength and weakness. Through testing one can determine the presence of a

learning disability and finally make recommendations for placement or an individual program of intervention. (Pierangelo and Giuliani, 1998, *Special Educator's Complete Guide to 109 Diagnostic Tests*) It is important to note here that in the mainstream school environment a professional is usually assigned to perform the assessment, and the educator's involvement is relegated to filling out a questionnaire, usually a rather long questionnaire, regarding the behavior of the child at school. However, if an educator can fill out the form, she can also develop for the school a rudimentary assessment process.

Any good early childhood teacher knows the importance of parent support. Parents hold in their memory the introduction and the first pages of the biography of the child that has just entered or is about to enter school: the birth, illnesses, developmental milestones, relationships, home environment—all of these bits of information form a picture of the child's life before entering school. Listening skills and good conferencing methods and a process for meeting the child are all that is needed to collect some of the information that supports the first stage of assessment.

The differences between the mainstream and a Waldorf inspired assessment process are what a Waldorf teacher finds important and how the teacher goes about collecting the information. It does not need to be clinical; there can be an artistic, warm and enthusiastic method for gathering this information.

Part two of the collection process involves classroom observation. When a child enters school, it is a valuable practice for the teacher to take up the task of observation each and every day. Observing a few children each day, using planned criteria and recording the observations until each and every child in the class has an entry, trains the ability to observe, can uncover surprising information and provides a baseline for writing year-end reports. In the first year of school it is important to observe how each child enters the classroom. It is important to determine the developmental appropriateness of the child's form and movement. As the child enters middle to upper kindergarten, observations of social development, relationship to work and play as well as physical development become important. We can see that when confronted by this first aspect of assessment — collection — that any teacher would use, a Waldorf teacher can garner a great deal of information about the children she is teaching through developing and managing a process of observation and record keeping.

When we consider the remainder of the mainstream process of assessment, analysis and evaluation, determination and recommendations, the picture is a little different. The thrust of the mainstream process is to determine if the child needs outside intervention, and that determination is made by analyzing the collected data and choosing, if it is appropriate, to request outside evaluative tests which will hopefully determine the problem and lead to recommendations of the appropriate interventions. This part of the process in a Waldorf school involves a heartfelt, meditative consideration of the information, asking the question: Why is this child behaving in this way? If the child is pinching, how is this child being pinched? As much as possible a Waldorf teacher continues to work within the framework of the classroom to provide interventions that do not isolate the child from the class. The thinking is, if an intervention is good for one child, it will probably benefit the entire class. Hopefully, there are other professionals on the staff of the school, a doctor, an educational support/extra lesson teacher, a curative eurythmist and sometimes other therapists, as well as colleagues who will provide support when the teacher thinks the child may need further assessment or intervention. But first the teacher must have a process for observation in place.

One of the Waldorf teacher's earliest criteria for observation involves early movement patterns. If even one child has not developed beyond these early movement patterns, then this child's need opens the door to providing movement opportunities for the whole class. These opportunities can be provided in the morning circle or during outdoor play. During these times the child can imitate and experience early movements such as expanding, contracting, rolling, pushing up, creeping, crawling, stretching and bending, as well as higher level movements such as jumping, hopping and skipping. Usually, Waldorf teachers provide the children with many opportunities to practice healthy movement sequences. However, the more conscious we become of the different aspects of developmental movement, the more we will be aware if a child is struggling or is hindered by a failure to develop skillfulness from a lower movement sequence to a higher one. All children need practice and reinforcement, but so much can be learned by simply choosing to observe certain aspects of the child's movement and recording observations.

Form is the other aspect available to the Waldorf teacher for observation. Children grow from the head into the limbs. The three-to-four year old is usually predominately head, with undifferentiated limbs. The head expresses a cosmic unity and gives the impression that the child is somewhat closed off or separate from the world. For example, the young child often plays alone or will start alone and warm to friendships from the safety of the snack table. They do not have true conversation at table, but more of a free association. What can be observed by the teacher is the above/below polarity of the form of the child. The healthy child is all head giving the impression of general roundness. However, more and more we see children who present different pictures. Some children are small, thin and wiry; often these children have limbs and hands that are weak. Some children are strong and round and heavy; often these children seem to be too big for the room or do not have a good sense of their strength and power. Another aspect of form involves the inherited body and how much or how little the child resembles one parent or the other. Children with older parents often have a distinct physical resemblance to a parent. Steiner spoke in the lectures on Curative Education of the importance of overcoming this inherited body. This can be more difficult when the parent is older and more material, and presents a baby with a body from that same material; a body that is rigid, less plastic and pliable. Steiner spoke of the need of the child to transform the inherited body to suit the needs of the individual soul and destiny (Steiner, 1998, pp.22–23). The more rigid the body is, the more hindered the child will be in this task. Education here can be either a remedy or a hindrance. An education that is not fixed and rigid can help in this first human task of making the body a home for the soul.

The young child can be observed from the standpoint of initial relationship to the environment, form, movement, and an independent holistic point of view. If the teacher would, as a practice, begin each day by choosing different aspects to observe and write a sentence or two about each child from the point of view of these different criteria, by the end of the year a school baseline picture should be clear.

Of course, as much as possible, all teachers need to train their observations. The younger the child, the more he is undergoing frequent change and growth. Young children just entering school are entirely condensed and undifferentiated. We speak of them as being a sense organ because they reflect and experience whatever is in the environment deeply. Older children can be more diversified, but up until the age of five, the little child is wide open. If you surround him with busyness and bright, coarse colors, he becomes all 'eye' and cannot separate himself from the visual input. This is naturally overwhelming. What does an overwhelmed child do? What does an adult do if truly overwhelmed but react? Why, if we as adults react, can we not accept that a child will do the same? An adult may maintain control by pinpointing the cause of her overwhelming experience and by compartmentalizing or exiting the environment; the young child cannot do this. Some children are overwhelmed by visual input, some by noise and others by smell; not all children in a class react to the same input. Some children are more sensitive to different types of environmental input, and it is very important to begin to observe how each child reacts to those different aspects of the environment.

I once had a five-year-old child in my class who was calm all morning until the food tray came into the room for lunch. He screamed and ran into the bathroom, slamming the door. The food on the tray was a stew with a combination of vegetables and meat. This child was sensitive to strong aromas. The rest of the children did not notice the aroma and could not understand why the sensitive child ran away. This experience initiated a conference with the child's parents, and together we came up with a classroom plan to help him overcome this sensitivity. The parents agreed to take him home for lunch. This was supposed to be a temporary solution, but the child was not able to join us for kindergarten lunch until the end of the school year. He was invited into the classroom early every morning before the other children arrived and before we started to cook any food. He was involved in all aspects of cooking, especially on days when soup was being made. Eventually his sensitivity to smell diminished, and by the end of the kindergarten year, although he carried his lunch from home, he was able to stay in the classroom for lunch without reacting to the aroma of the food as it was brought into the room.

Components of
Human Development

The Four Bodies of the Human Being

Rudolf Steiner offers us a complex and comprehensive picture of how the human being is incorporated into his body. The human being is composed of four bodies: physical, etheric, astral and ego. The physical body we can see and touch is related to the mineral; the other three bodies can be seen, but are not necessarily visible in the same way as the physical body. A great gift of living or working with young children is that, as the child grows and develops, one can gain glimpses or become conscious through observation of human components that we typically do not see. The etheric body can be made visible through growth, upward movement and the expression of health and well-being or vitality, a rosy glow. The astral body can be made visible in relationships, first to the environment and in the manner the child breathes in the world and lets it go and in the child's relationship to consciousness and unconsciousness in sleeping and waking, in the ability to mimic or imitate and in the quality the child expresses in speaking. Finally, once the child has overcome gravity, stood upright and learned to speak, then the ego body asserts itself from within and the child can say, "I." The warmth of the ego is at first self-centered or selfish. This fire of making the body home for the soul, and the ego consciously living within it can be seen in the demands for independence of the two- to three-year- old. This can give the ego body visibility.

If we wish to train our eye to see the etheric body, we must train ourselves to think of the effect of the etheric body in one who is newly born. In the newborn child, the etheric body makes itself known through movement and the first breath which transforms the color of the skin. It gives the child a quality of life and liveliness. Through it we can judge the well-being and aliveness of the newborn. When we die, the etheric body separates from the physical, thus allowing the physical its stony element. A dead person appears stony and fixed. Life is color and movement. Through the etheric body the human being is related to the plant world which expresses life in its greenness and movement in growth.

Through the astral body, the human being is related to the animal world. Animals are instinctive creatures. When a child prepares for birth through the early months of life, survival is dependent on attachment. The astral body makes itself known through all the instinctive movements the infant makes to bring itself to uprightness, through the imitative role it takes on in relationship to the surrounding world, and through the experience the child gains through the senses of touch with beginning exploration. The child experiences the beginning of a feeling life through imitation. By imitating expressions of feeling in the surrounding world through a relationship with parents or caregivers, the child explores the life of feelings. The closest the human being comes to the instinctual aspect of the animal is the bodily based, early movement patterns which bond the child to care givers who protect and give nourishment. The difference is that these movements become inhibited when the human being overcomes gravity, stands upright and takes on distinctly human characteristics.

The ego body, which is connected to yet higher and developing aspects of the human being, is that seed of self that rules our awareness of our being, so that we are something more than purely a physical-being related to the earth, or a life-being related to the plants, or an instinctive-sense being related to the animals. The ego works primarily outside of the body of the developing human being. This ego body makes itself known through warmth and self-consciousness. The warmth of the body is something that requires ongoing protection until the child is much older. At first the newborn spends most of this time sleeping, and even when the baby is awake, one cannot be certain about the quality of the child's consciousness other than it is somewhat plant-like. The newborn is certainly not conscious in the same way an adult is conscious. The newborn dreams into life. (Steiner, 1996a, p.41)

Then the child begins to move. The child's first movements enable him to explore his body and the surrounding world of his family. These initial explorations give way to movements that gradually bring the child into an upright posture and free movement. Now the child can explore the surrounding environment. The child strikes out in his explorations under the care and guidance of his loving family. Through imitation speech becomes the new frontier and quickly, if all is well with the child, he begins to play at speech.

Once the child enters into the world through movement and speech, he meets resistance. The child has a very rudimentary experience of being something other than the world in which he is exploring. This true sense of self is not firmly incorporated until the age of nine. Only after nine can the child really begin to own and name an experience with the feeling life of the soul. However, the ego body makes itself known along the way. We can recognize the beginning of the incorporation of the ego body at the moment the child is heard to say 'I' when speaking of himself; only a human being can speak 'I' of himself. At this moment the child becomes human and related to the earth, and the ego or being of man begins working from within.

These are the four bodies of the human being made visible through thoughtful observation of a child's growth. Scientists have also observed the activity of these bodies. For example, in the middle of the last century Dr. Virginia Apgar developed a test which was named after her and continues to be the first test and score the human being must take and pass in almost any type of medical setting after birth. (Apgar, 1953) Dr. Apgar originally developed this test for research purposes to assess the effects of different birthing presentations and procedures, such as anesthesia, forceps, and surgery on the health of the newborn infant. The assessment is twofold and is characterized first by breathing time and crying time and then by five objective signs assessed within one minute after birth: heart rate, respiratory effort, reflex irritability, muscle tone and color. This medical test assesses the relationship of the soul to the physical body through heart rate and breathing, the relationship of the etheric body to the physical body through tone and color, and the relationship of the astral body  to the etheric through reflex irritability or muscle instinct. What a doctor needs to know at the time of birth to determine the health of the child can actually guide us to observe the activity of the four bodies of the human being that Steiner so eloquently described.

Studies of the four bodies offer us a picture of how the human being is formed. The human being is more than a physical body. Throughout the whole of life, she or he expresses capacities which are the seeds of different aspects of the higher human being. These capacities can be described as they develop through three seven year cycles.

The Threefold Human Being

The capacities of the healthy human being that are developed throughout the three seven-year cycles are thinking, feeling and willing. Thinking is connected to the nerves and senses, feeling to the rhythmic system, and willing to the limbs and digestion. As the child grows, these capacities of the soul are built and balanced. All three are connected and develop over each seven-year cycle but in each cycle one capacity at a time is the focus for development. In the early childhood years from ages three to seven, while the metabolism and limb systems are developing and maturing, the capacity of the will is the focus. From ages seven to fourteen, the feeling life and the rhythmic system are the focus of the child's development. From ages fourteen to twenty-one, the capacity of thinking and the nerves and sense organs mature.

It is important to point out here that once the human being enters the realm of these three soul capacities, thinking, feeling and willing, he firmly leaves behind the kingdom of animals. The animal cannot think, feel compassion, or will through intention. The ego has entered the body at age two-and-a-half or three, and beginning from that moment the long development of the soul begins. Waldorf education is an education for the soul and these three capacities are human soul capacities.

Breathing

The movement and balance between these three capacities comes about through breathing and the organs of the senses. When a child is born the first thing the child does is take a breath. Breathing is the first physical activity all of us take part in upon entering life on earth. Taking a breath and breathing are two different things. The child has been surrounded by a watery world in the womb and any experience of breathing is due to the fetal connection to the mother's own breathing. Being born means that the child moves from a watery world to an airy world, and from living in total relationship to the mother to semi- or helpless independence. A newborn baby is simply cast into a world where the main element of life, air, is a substance that could not be more foreign to the child. The fact that a newborn can make this transition at all is a miracle and one of those awe-inspiring moments in the life of any adult involved in any birth.

Breathing is a rhythmic relationship between inner and outer, point and periphery, expansion and contraction. Breathing in is related to the present, current and earthly human. Breathing out is related to the cosmic whole, both past and future. When Steiner speaks of the importance of the breathing process, this relationship which takes place within the human being, he also describes it as an activity that one must learn. (Steiner, 1996a, p.41) Through breathing we take in and relate to the outer physical world, and it is an activity that makes it possible for the 'I' or spirit to be incorporated into the body by developing a relationship in which the threefold system of the human body is drawn together harmoniously. Through the middle system, the rhythmic system, both the nerve/sense system and metabolic/limb system are brought into relatedness and harmonious balance. The three parts of the human being are entirely penetrated by breathing.

During an in-breath, the cerebral-spinal fluid bathes the brain and during an out-breath, it is drawn back into the body. The rhythm of breathing also has an impact on the movement of the limbs and digestion. Through breathing blood circulation is connected to the metabolic process and the blood is entirely responsible for assimilation of the outer world into the physical body taken in through the digestive process. If you observe that a child is too awake or too asleep, or that the child's movement is not rhythmical or harmonious, or that the child has poor digestion, you can trace the cause directly to a lack of harmony and rhythm in the child's breathing. "When we bring the breathing into harmony with the nerve-sense process, then we draw the spirit-soul into the child's physical life. Roughly stated, we can say that children cannot yet of themselves breathe properly, and that education consists in teaching proper breathing." (Steiner, 1996a, pp.40–41)

Waking and Sleeping

Along the same lines, the child begins to incorporate a right rhythm in sleeping and waking. Sleeping and waking are similar to in-breathing and out-breathing in several ways. First of all sleeping and waking is a process that a child must learn. Young children do not sleep in the same manner as adults. They do not take in the world in sleep, process it and transform it. Instead, they dream into the spiritual world. Since the young child is so informed then by the spiritual world, we parents and teachers have very little to teach young children that they can take in and digest. Rather, we have the task to help them find a right relationship between sleeping and waking. We provide the right environment, the right rhythm and the right attitude to meet the needs of the young child. Secondly,

sleeping and waking are polarities which have a rhythmic relationship to the nerves and senses system that is conscious or awake and to metabolism which is unconscious or asleep. Balance between sleeping and waking is crucial to the development of thinking. If the child is too awake or too asleep, he cannot create within himself an environment for growth and development through education. Finally, the three systems of the human being — and through them the world — are penetrated by the ego by letting go and engaging through sleeping and waking. (Steiner, 1996a, p.41)

Studies of the brain are beginning to substantiate the importance of this relationship between sleeping and waking. The hippocampus, which is a part of the brain that extends into both hemispheres, appears to be the hub for learning and memory. It does not store individual memories but rather sorts memories, filters what is important to include or ignore, and makes new associations. Recent experiments point to the important role sleep and particularly dreaming have in the process of memory. "Recent experiments also show that sleep, specifically the sleep associated with dreaming, is important to human memory. In Israel, researchers Avi Karni and Dov Sagi at the Weizmann Institute found that interrupting REM sleep sixty times in a night completely blocked learning, but interrupting non-REM sleep just as often did not. These findings and others suggest that REM sleep is crucial for organizing pieces and the associations between them needed for forming lasting memories."(Ratey, 2002, pp.188-189)

Audrey McAllen devoted much of her life to developing exercises based on the indications Steiner gave as the teacher's task in teaching children to breathe and sleep harmoniously. (Steiner, 1996a, p.42) "The sleep environment of the child's soul is the 'after echo' of the daily experiences working in the body of formative forces and thence harmoniously or disturbingly into the physical body." (McAllen, 2004, p.35)

During the first seven years of life, children take into themselves everything they are exposed to with absolute devotion, particularly through the physical senses. "Their whole sensory system grasps hold of the world they live in." (McAllen, 2004, p.33) If the child is exposed to too much stimuli in the surrounding environment or through our teaching, sleep will be disturbed. If sleep is disturbed, then memory, an element of learning, is also challenged.

The Organs of the Senses

Steiner expanded our understanding of the human experience by providing us with a picture of twelve senses to perceive the world around us: sense of life, sense of movement, sense of balance, sense of touch, sense of smell, sense of taste, sense of sight, sense of warmth, sense of hearing, word sense, sense of thought, and ego sense. As he developed his ideas of the human sense world, he did not initially consider the sense of touch a separate sense. Rather he described it as an activity that was involved in all of the senses. Later in his work he included touch as one of the lower or foundation senses. He explored the senses in many ways, for example, in hierarchical order or as polarities across the circle of the senses. As an example, if we view them in polarity, the sense of touch is opposite the sense of ego. The sense of touch allows the human being to determine boundaries, while the ego sense breaks into the boundaries of another. (Soesman, 2000, p.145) The sense of touch is one of our first organs of sense, and the ego sense is the last to develop. In some ways touch is a sense that makes us more earthbound or world-related, and the sense of ego is unique to the upright, independent, human being.

Steiner worked his entire adult life to develop the picture of the human senses. He viewed the acquisition and maturity of the twelve senses to be vitally important to a healthy relationship with the world. It is through the senses the human being penetrates and comes to understand the world and ultimately takes up his place in it. Through the twelve senses the human being is able to perceive the world in its many aspects — color, movement, sights and sounds — and re-member or re-unite the parts into a whole. (Steiner, 1996a, pp.144–45) Sense perceptions experienced through the healthy, developed organs train the thinking and judgment of the human being.

The capacity to think comes alive because the different perceptions of the world, which are received through the organs of the senses, force the human being to unite with the world or make a connection to it. For example, when we smell, we take in something of the surrounding environment (the world), we experience it inwardly, and we react to it through sympathy or antipathy, attraction or revulsion. We may take some sort of action based on our perception of the sensation, such as stay in or leave the room. A surprising quote from a recent book, *A User's Guide to the Brain* by Dr. John Ratey, a professor of Psychiatry at Harvard University, supports this view: "Human experience begins with information about the world that flows in through our senses, but depends on how the information

is combined with internal states to produce action." Although Dr. Ratey's focus is more on the actual motor activity, the fact that he has this view affirms Steiner's view that the senses connect us to the world and that the information is combined or put together internally within the human being. Perception through the senses leads to action or inaction.

The organs of the twelve senses develop throughout childhood up until the age of twenty-one. Each of the three cycles is a phase for the development of a particular set of four of the twelve senses: birth to seven, the four lower senses — life, touch, balance and movement; seven to fourteen, the middle senses — smell, taste, sight and warmth; and fourteen to twenty-one, the higher senses — hearing, word, thought and ego. The maturing of the senses allotted to each of these phases depends upon the healthy development during the previous phase. As an example, sight depends on a relationship to balance and movement which is developed in the first phase of early childhood. Although this may be difficult to grasp, conventional science has well documented this connection. For an annotated bibliography of some of this research, see Appendix A.

Children in non-Waldorf schools are being asked in early childhood settings to sit more than an hour at a time and complete worksheets. The belief is that the more you practice test-taking skills, the more likely you are to score higher on standardized tests. Children in these schools do have movement breaks, but these breaks are often not opportunities for free movement. In time at school then, children are given fewer and fewer opportunities to practice balance and movement. In the introduction of her book *Reflexes, Learning and Behavior*, p.xvi, Sally Goddard states: "Movement lies at the heart of learning. Learning, language and behaviors are all linked in some way to the function of the motor system and control of movement."

Karl König founded the Camphill movement for disabled children. In one of his lectures he spoke of the act of writing: "If we turn now to the act of writing, we will find that it is one of the most complicated and hidden of all human activities. In writing the ear is replaced by the eye because writing is a kind of speaking, not with mouth and larynx, but with eye and hand. Writing has two main sources: the eye and everything that is connected to it, and the motor activity of arm, hand and fingers." (König, 2002, p.33). The eye, which is an organ of the middle senses, does not mature until the middle years of childhood, elementary school, but in order to write, the arm and hand need to be mature and ready to support the eye with free movement. If children are not given the opportunity to develop this free movement, then there will be a breakdown in skill and capacity for writing. Further, there is a movement component to eyesight: expansion/contraction, touch, etc. If the child does not have the ability to move in a general or gross motor realm, how can we expect him to develop skill in the specific or fine motor realm? An interesting study could come about by observing the effect on eyesight and hearing when children are not allowed to move for hours on end. There are certainly enough opportunities for this sort of research in non-Waldorf school settings.

Currently in non-Waldorf school settings, the lower senses — movement, balance and will — are not often incorporated into the curriculum or even considered to be supportive to academic work. The will is spoken of as will-power, or strong will, but not as a capacity that is paramount to human development and that enables the individual to be educated. On the other hand, Stanley Greenspan and T. Berry Brazelton have written much on the feeling life of children; Jean Piaget studied and wrote about the cognitive development of children; and Rudolf Steiner viewed the development and maturity of the will as an aspect important to the education of the child. Steiner also speaks about a relationship between will and feeling in the young child. In *The Foundations of Human Experience*, p.123, he says, "When children kick or wiggle, they make exactly those movements that reflect their feelings at that moment. The child is unable to separate movement [which is a 'will' sense] from feeling." If the child cannot make appropriate boundaries through a healthy touch sense, then the entire day is about failed interactions with others. If the child cannot stand upright and relate to the world in a balanced manner and move through the world, then reading and writing and all of the middle senses — sight, smell, taste and hearing — will be delayed or impaired in the early years of elementary school. "For too long teachers have concentrated upon the psychological problems of the child, or the socio-economic environment, instead of asking the question, does the child have the equipment which he needs to succeed at the educational level asked of him and the methods imposed on him." (Goddard, 2002, p.131) Movement and balance are currently being considered in mainstream thought for addition to the sensory picture, especially as neurologists study the brain and occupational therapists explore the difficulties some children have with tactile sensitivity or reactivity related to it and difficulties with balance and movement.

In the early 1970s Jane Ayres, an occupational therapist who worked with neurologically disabled children and adults, described the proprioception sense and the vestibular sense. She described the proprioception sense as being "the sensation caused by contracting and stretching of muscles and by bending, straightening, pulling and compression of the joints between bones. Sheaths that cover the bones also contain proprioceptors. The term comes from the Latin word 'proprius' meaning one's own. The sensations from one's own body occur especially during movement; but they also occur while we are standing still, for the muscles and joints constantly send information to the brain to tell us about our position." (Ayres, 2000, p.35) Ayres described the vestibular sense as that sense which "tells us exactly where we are in relationship to gravity, whether we are moving or still, and how fast we are going and in what direction."(Ayres, 2000, p.36) This relationship is determined by gravity receptors and the semi-circular canals in the inner ear and how information they receive is processed in the brain.

As the focus of this book is an assessment or process for observation during the years of early childhood education, the four lower senses are of primary consideration. That is not to say the other senses, particularly the middle senses (sight, smell, taste and hearing) cannot be observed. A young child sees, smells, tastes, and hears, but these sensations are experienced only after birth. They are new to the child in each environmental experience; initially the child cannot differentiate between different types of sensations because the organs are still developing and differentiating. A young child focuses on sense experiences one sense at a time, becoming entirely

given over to a taste sensation or a smell sensation. Because young children sense the world with their entire beings, they become all eye when the most intense experience is color and they become all nose when the most intense experience is smell. These sensations are in the exploratory range for young children.

On the other hand, the four lower senses are at a different level of maturity than the middle senses, because the child has experience with touch, life, movement and balance in the womb. If we look at the first concrete activity of being born, breathing, the infant must have a relationship to movement and balance in some rudimentary way in order to take a breath and to maintain an initial and albeit un-rhythmical balance between in-breathing and out-breathing. Further, after taking a first breath the health (sense of life) of the child is judged by the heartiness of the sound of his cry, his color, his ability to suckle or respond to touch and movement. (Apgar, 1953) Immediately upon joining the physical world, the child is judged through observation of the lower senses – the senses of life, movement, balance and touch.

When the newborn enters the world, these four lower senses provide the gateway and support for their survival needs. Beyond survival, without active and healthy lower senses, the infant will not thrive in a way that will allow for healthy growth and development, and this will have an impact on the child's ability to learn and enter life as a human being free to live and act in the world. As the child begins to move in the world, "they explore space, first crawling on hands and knees, a stage which experience has shown is vital for the development of the coordination system on which the depends the development of writing and reading skills." (McAllen, 2004, pp.35–36)

The four lower senses are necessary to the maturity of the other eight senses. Balance and movement are necessary to seeing, hearing, smelling and tasting. The eye 'sees' an object by moving around the object with the eye (movement), adapting to light by expansion and contraction of the lens (balance). Health and attention can also be observed in the eyes (life).

Steiner called the four lower senses the senses of will. The will, as an independent capacity, is active and not conscious of the intention to act. If we look at the young child we could observe a will-driven nature. If healthy, the young child is active and unconscious of what drives those actions. If you ask young children why they misbehave or strike another child, they do not know. If you ask them why they are playing, they do not know. They are not conscious of their intention even if we adults think we can understand 'why' they are acting in a certain manner.

The four lower senses give the child the power to overcome gravity and penetrate and transform the physical structure. Through the sense perceptions the child learns to make his body his home. All of the senses inform the child about the environment and the earth, but the four lower senses inform the child about himself.

To understand this world of the senses and make use of that understanding as a teacher, one must first have a very rudimentary understanding of how the child enters the world. What do we see first in the infant? We see a unity, an entire universe in the cosmic and singular roundness of the head. The limbs seem to be an afterthought. They are soft and flailing, not penetrated or under the control of the child. Most animals are born with the instincts to be capable adults within the first year of life. The human being takes years to develop, twenty-one years to be exact. Steiner described those twenty-one years in three seven-year periods, and within that time the human soul must penetrate first the physical body in the first seven years, the rhythmic system during the second seven years, and finally the

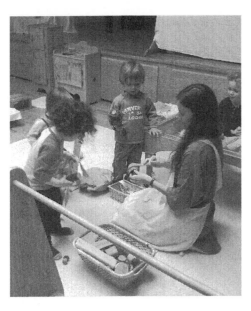

nerves and senses in the third seven years.

In the first seven-year period the surrounding environment is entirely penetrating the child with all of its force. The ego of the child must gradually learn to meet the environment through its own will forces and to take up the physical body. At first the child seems to dream into life (Steiner, 1996a, p.41), asleep more than awake. The infant is not yet related to the world in any sort of conscious manner. The length of this time often depends on the quality of the child's entrance into the world. If he had a normal birth process and was allowed bonding time, the child's connection to the world of the family will be more concrete. A child who was born by Caesarian-section often seems to hover in a placid 'womb' state; while a traumatic or stressed birth experience will require time for healing. The birth process awakens and connects the child to the world he is being born into, namely his family.

Why is this important? Because the well being of the child is related to the etheric or life body and it is within this body all the cosmic forms and rhythms for growth are living. The etheric realm is related to the plant world. The plant grows into a form that is wise and lawful. Its growth is rhythmic, with the leaves appearing at intervals and its development universal, or expressing patterns of growth that repeat in every plant. The human being has an important connection to this universal etheric body, and the more the child is protected within it, the more quickly and easily he relates to the world he has entered.

The Reflexes or Early Movement Patterns

Beginning with the birth process itself, we can observe universal movement patterns that develop in the womb, enable the child to enter and move through the birth canal and ultimately guide the child to uprightness and movement in the world. These movement patterns are commonly referred to as the developmental reflexes.

From the most primitive to the most complex, the immature movement patterns are: Moro reflex, palmar and plantar reflexes, asymmetric tonic neck reflex (ATNR), rooting reflex, spinal Galant, tonic labyrinthine reflex (TLR), and the symmetrical tonic neck reflex (STNR). The birth process reinforces ATNR and all of the reflexes so that they are established and available during the first months of life as a bridge to higher level patterns of movement or skills.

The developmental milestones of creeping, crawling, sitting, standing, walking and speaking depend on the presence, healthy development and eventual integration and inhibition of these early movement patterns. Studies have shown that these immature movement patterns are hierarchical and limited in their useful life. "The inhibition of a reflex frequently correlates with the acquisition of a new skill." (Goddard, 2002, p.2) If the presence of the early movement patterns extends beyond certain developmental periods or fails to support purposeful development, this signals neuro-developmental delay. Physical and behavioral hindrances are the outcome of a failure to overcome these early movement patterns. These hindrances point us in the direction of the movement pattern(s) responsible for the delay and can guide and structure remediation.

In the first weeks after conception the fetus can be tested and made to react to stimulation beginning with touch of the upper lip and moving gradually over the entire surface of the body. The fetus reacts to touch by withdrawing or moving away from the stimulus. As tactile awareness becomes more general, the withdrawal reaction lessens. One could say that tactile awareness is the first 'skill' that the fetus learns that overcomes the most primitive or basic reaction. From the beginning of the development of these early movement patterns, the progression is based on the acquisition of previous 'skills,' and their inhibition will also be dependent upon acquisition of new skills.

The Moro reflex is the first of the immature movement patterns to emerge, at around nine to twelve weeks after conception. *In utero*, the Moro reflex is thought to play a role in preparing the breathing mechanism and at birth for stimulating the first breath and helping to open the newborn's windpipe. (Goddard, 2002, p.5) After birth the Moro reflex is "an involuntary reaction to threat, a survival mechanism that alerts, arouses and causes a reaction that summons help." (Goddard, 2002, p.5) It must be pointed out again and again that all stimuli are new and therefore 'sudden' to the newborn. The newborn cannot 'analyze' and assess or determine if the stimuli is a threat. Just as the fetus reacts to all touch stimuli until nine to twelve weeks *in utero*, the newborn infant with the protection of the Moro reflex, reacts to all tactile (touch), visual, auditory or vestibular stimuli.

The Moro reflex initiates arousal through a series of movements. The arms move upward and outward or away from the body with open hands. There is a momentary freeze and the arms and hands contract in a clasping gesture. The outward movement (expansion) is accompanied by an in-breath, and the inward movement (contraction) is accompanied by an out-breath.

Through arousal of the Moro reflex, the sympathetic nervous system develops and with practice overtakes the role of the reflex which should be inhibited by two to four months of life. If the reflex is not inhibited the child will startle easily, show hypersensitivity to sensory stimuli, and may have irregular breathing patterns.

The Moro reflex is the most basic of the immature movement patterns. It is the first movement pattern to develop and extremely important to the survival of the infant. The other early movement patterns develop out of the Moro reflex and if symptoms of any of the higher patterns exist, it is assumed that the Moro reflex has not been inhibited. All the early movement patterns are important and have an impact on development and if not inhibited can be responsible for educational delays.

The palmar and plantar reflexes emerge around eleven weeks *in utero*, should be fully present at birth and inhibited at two to three months of life. They are reactions to touch stimulus. They respond as part of the movement pattern of the arousal of the Moro reflex. When the palm of the hand or the sole of the foot is gently stroked, the hand grasps or the foot curls. These reflexes are "thought to be a continuation of an earlier stage of evolution" when it was necessary to "cling to the mother for survival."(Goddard, 2002, p.8)

The palmar reflex will react involuntarily when the child sucks (Babkin response). There is a relationship between the mouth and hands. If this reflex is not inhibited, further development of manual dexterity and speech formation may result. If the palmar reflex is not inhibited, independent thumb and finger movement are not possible and the ability to hold an object, and eventually a pencil, will be impaired. Since a relationship can be observed between sucking and grasping, proper formation in speech may prove impossible. 'Overflow' or movements of the mouth when a child is learning to write, is a sign of an active palmar reflex.

Asymmetrical tonic neck reflex emerges at eighteen weeks *in utero*, should be fully present at birth and inhibited at six months of life. Head movement from side to side stimulates this early movement pattern. When the head of the baby turns to the left, the left leg will stretch and the right leg will flex; when the head turns to the right, the right leg will stretch and the left leg will flex. "*In utero* this movement pattern facilitates movement (the kick), develops muscle tone and provides vestibular (balance) stimulation." (Goddard, 2002, p.10) ATNR participates in the birth process enabling the baby to move through the birth canal, adjusting to the rhythm of labor.

This early movement pattern, along with the Moro reflex, is crucial to the early survival of the newborn child. The ATNR causes the newborn to turn his head from side to side while in the prone position, thus facilitating breathing. It also develops muscle tone one side at a time and allows for the beginning of eye/hand coordination. If it is not inhibited at six months, it will interfere with the development of more complex skills and it will be difficult for the child to overcome the vertical midline barrier. The midline barrier is useful for development; without it the child would not use both hands and might grow dependent on just one chosen side of the body. "This barrier remains active until about age six or seven. It is at this time that handedness is firmly established, and the brain is undergoing a growth spurt that triggers the transformations leading to concrete thinking. The body is readying itself for the vast array of asymmetrical tasks that lie ahead."(Coulter, 1999, p.63) If ATNR were to remain in place, it would be impossible for the child to crawl or eventually walk in a cross pattern movement, upright balance would be insecure, and passing an object from one hand to the other (crossing the vertical midline) would be difficult if not impossible.

The rooting reflex emerges around twenty-four to twenty-eight weeks *in utero*, is fully present at birth and should be inhibited by three to four months of life. This early movement pattern is stimulated by stroking the cheek of the infant and will cause the baby to turn its head toward the stimulus, open its mouth and extend its tongue in preparation to suck or nurse. This reflex is strongest in the early hours after birth, and if not stimulated it will diminish. This reflex is crucial to successful nursing in the early days of life. An uninhibited or retained rooting reflex can lead to difficulty in eating (chewing and swallowing) and with speech articulation. Since the rooting reflex is also related to the palmar reflex, the child may have poor manual dexterity if either of these movement patterns is impaired or retained.

The spinal Galant reflecx emerges around twenty weeks *in utero*, is actively present at birth and should be inhibited at three to nine months of life. When the baby is placed face down (prone) and the area to the right or left of the spine is gently stroked, the baby will lift and rotate the hip forty-five degrees on the same side toward the stimulus. If both sides of the spine are stimulated, the Pulgar

Marx reflex is elicited; the movement involves flexion of both legs, elevation of the pelvis and emptying of the bladder or movement of the bowels. It is believed this reflex is useful during birth and like the ATNR helps the baby move and adapt during the birth process. Little is known about this reflex, but if it is not inhibited, it may be responsible for bed wetting, inability to control movement (fidgeting) and poor coordination.

The tonic labyrinthine reflex has two aspects: The forward TLR emerges *in utero* and is responsible for the fetal position posture. This posture should be inhibited by four months of life. The backward TLR emerges at birth and engages the head of the fetus in the birth canal. The extended TLR should be inhibited by approximately six months of life or once the baby has established control of the head. TLR is linked to the Moro in the early months of life. Both are vestibular in origin and are "activated by stimulation of the labyrinths, movement of the head and alteration of position in space." (Goddard, 2002, p.17)

TLR provides balance between the womb and the world. This early movement pattern allows the infant to stretch out of the fetal position and develop muscle tone that will eventually allow the child to take control of the head. If the child cannot grow out of this early movement pattern, internal balance will be severely affected, and the child will have difficulty navigating and processing visually, spatially, sequentially.

Symmetrical tonic neck reflex or STNR emerges at around six to nine months of life and should be inhibited by nine to eleven months of life. This early movement pattern also has two aspects, flexion and extension. When the child is on all fours, flexion of the head causes the arms to bend and the legs to extend. When the child pushes the head up into extension, this causes the legs to flex and the arms to straighten. (Goddard, 2002, p.21) Since this reflex does not emerge *in utero* or at birth, it is not considered a primitive reflex, but instead bridges the gap between early established survival patterning movements and more developed movement such as creeping, crawling, standing, walking, etc. It is a reflex through which the infant can establish a posture that will overcome the prone position and gravity. Without the help of STNR, which can emerge only if the other early movement patterns are in place, and ten without its eventual inhibition through practice of higher level movement patterns such as crawling, an upright posture, balance and coordination will be adversely affected.

These early movement patterns have a time and place in the embryonic and early life of the human being. They are related and develop out of each other, and they are of necessity inhibited by higher movement and normal development. Many children today have issues with retention of one or more of these early movement patterns. The reasons for these challenges are multiple, beginning with pregnancy and extending into environmental and parenting practices. Many of the behaviors and weaknesses children present in school can be directly linked to a failure to move beyond these patterns and, yet again, a failure to give the child free movement opportunities.

Jane Swain is a pediatric physical therapist and an associate director of Sophia's Hearth Family Center in Keene, New Hampshire. She has studied especially the work of Emmi Pikler,

whose Pikler Institute offers parent-child classes to support the healthy development of children. and also runs an orphanage in Budapest, Hungary. Jane Swain visited there to observe their care-giving practices. Among other things the infants are given extensive opportunities for 'self-initiated' activity or movement. Jane Swain comments that she "did not see abnormal retention of the primitive reflexes." When she inquired about the retention of the reflexes, the staff said: "This is not an issue." Not so in almost every classroom in America, where it is quite unusual *not* to see symptoms of retained reflexes. Sadly, retained early movement patterns are becoming pervasive in this country, often simply a symptom of the failure to provide infants and children time to move freely. (Swain, 2008)

This concludes the first part of this book in which the effort has been to develop the aspects of child development out of both Rudolf Steiner's picture and from current ongoing scientific and educational studies. The remainder of the book is devoted to a plan for assessment which a teacher can maintain in the classroom.

THE BEGINNING OF SCHOOL

The Early Childhood Program

School is mandatory after age six, but many children begin school between ages three and six. Why do parents send young children to school? Early Childhood programs exist mainly because parents are either seeking a community where they can meet other parents and share their parenting experiences, or they need childcare for their children, or more recently because they view early childhood programs as a gateway to a better education. Since these needs and views are unlikely to change in the near future, it is important to develop a picture of what a healthy school environment might be for the young child.

Rudolf Steiner outlines the needs of the growing child: "Up to the seventh year, approximately, i.e., up to the change of teeth, we find the education must proceed from imitation, the child's impulse to imitate. In my booklet, *The Education of the Child in the Light of Anthroposophy*, I emphasize that what the child sees and hears from the adults in his environment in these first years is far more important for his education than all moral rules and other forms of instruction." For the period after the change of teeth and before puberty, Steiner continues, "By freeing ourselves from all prejudices and looking purely at actual human development and its requirements, we find the most important educational impulse at this time is what we call authority. A healthy education for this period of life comes about when the child is in the presence of adults whom he can trust and believe, and when he can form his principles and rules of conduct on the authority of those adults who are close to him. This must occur without any pale, intellectual ideas and without demanding from the child an unripe critical faculty." For the period between puberty and young adulthood, Steiner declares, "The most important condition for human development to be the maturing of the intellect, and especially the ability to look up to an impersonal ideal in one's soul, that is, to a purely spiritual educational impulse, one which stands above what the human being can be at this age." (Steiner, 1995, pp.1–3)

Since the *No Child Left Behind Act* was instituted (in 2001), the emphasis in early education has been on teaching children to read and write earlier so that they can pass standardized tests successfully during elementary school.

> The purpose of this title [No Child Left Behind Act] is to ensure that all children have a fair, equal, and significant opportunity to obtain a high-quality education and reach, at a minimum, proficiency on challenging State academic achievement standards and state academic assessments. (Ed.Gov. – United States Department of Education)

This Act has placed the education of children squarely in the hands of politicians who are mandating earlier and earlier testing of children for reading and math on federal, state and citywide levels. What capacities are required for successful test taking? Besides reading and writing and the ability to follow directions, critical thinking and a developed ability to judge between multiple answers are necessary to answer test questions successfully. The ability to sit quietly and remain focused during a time sequence of at least twenty minutes is required, as is an emotional security to deal with the regimental delivery of test instructions. In the current educational climate ruled by the *No Child Left Behind Act*, young children are expected to use capacities that they have not yet developed, let alone learned to use.

Children are expected to be capable of critical thinking before the maturing of the intellect. Nor is there recognition that thinking is a learned capacity and that children are maturing and growing into capacities during childhood. There is merely a token recognition that children can have developmental differences and individual learning styles that may complicate standardized test-taking and, therefore, scores. Those determining the form of education, as it now stands, assume that training of the intellect is its primary task. They do not take into account how or when a child learns the capacity of judgment nor do they recognize the role of imitation in the education of the child.

According to Steiner, children who go to school between birth and the change of teeth should be met with an education that depends on upon the 'impulse to imitate.' Restated, the impulse is for imitation and not authority. Authority becomes the impulse of the education of the child after the change of teeth. What does an early childhood classroom look like? What are the characteristics of a teacher who stands before the young child in whom imitation is the active learning impulse? What are the characteristics of a program that supports the development of the young child?

Let us look again at the picture of human development that was outlined in the first half of this book, namely, that the human being's first activity upon birth is to take a breath and awaken into the world; that the human being has four developing bodies (physical, etheric, astral, spirit) which are maturing through the years and ripening at specific points in the human biography; that the human being is also a threefold being with a body, soul and spirit and three capacities for earth life, thinking, feeling and willing which develop a bond to the earth. The human being is being nurtured through the senses that also represent developing organs which can be developed either wrongly or not at all, or through healthy means. And finally, the human being has a need to move through early movement patterns to overcome gravity and become human. The early childhood environment must therefore take into account all of these criteria for the healthy maturing of the child.

The classroom is first and foremost the environment for the education of the child. Of course the environment is produced by human beings, the teacher(s) and sometimes the parents, but it is important that the early childhood classroom be an environment that is beautiful, peaceful, safe and sensory rich (not sensory overwhelming). Although the early childhood classroom can hum rather noisily internally, it is important that the classroom itself be protected from noise and painted with soft colors and that the toys and furnishings are of natural materials, and the colors, smells and textures do not assault the senses. Rather, the senses must find  the environment inviting, interesting and appealing. There needs to be space to move and time for different experiences of movement such as those provided by both indoor and outdoor play. The toys must provide the children with a means of imitating the activity in the classroom and take into account the different needs of the ages of the children.

Since children need basically the environment of the home at this age, the school environment typically should imitate the most positive of home activities: helping the child towards independence in self care, learning to cook and make bread, working together to keep the house clean and a complementary time for play and interesting craft activities. If the kindergarten is imitative of home life, then the children in the early childhood years should be surrounded by a family represented by children of different ages. Children learn from each other, and a mixed age kindergarten provides many opportunities for such learning. A mixed-age kindergarten, beginning when the child is ready to separate (usually around age three), if the law allows, until the change of teeth would be the most supportive environment for the young child.

The best model for the teaching staff in early childhood is the team approach rather than the lead teacher/assistant. The lead teacher/ assistant model belongs in the realm of the elementary school and the principle of authority rather than the principle of imitation. One problem between the lead teacher and assistant in the kindergarten might have to do with salary. Other than possibly higher increments for experience or training, the base salary of the teachers in the kindergarten classroom should be the same. The needs of a teacher who is learning or developing should be met through adequate student teaching and internships. But active kindergarten teachers should be paid the same and have similar work expectations. The number of teachers in the classroom could be determined by both the number of children and the ages of the children in the classroom. The children who are three have different needs than the children who are four, and each teacher could take the lead by working with a specific age group. All of the teachers in the class should come to know all of the children through opportunities for observation and study. A team approach offers a wonderful opportunity for child care and child study within the mixed age group. The team approach also makes the mixed age group much more manageable and successful. Certainly teamwork requires a different process and skills of management, communication and interaction. However, since the impulse of imitation demands the children see adults working together cooperatively on meeting their needs and forming the classroom, team teaching offers an excellent opportunity for creating an example worthy of imitation.

Since the impulse to imitate is what trains the will, the will is the capacity which the child is developing during the early childhood years. The teachers of young children have a deeply important task to consider, namely preparing themselves to be worthy of imitation. This task calls upon the teacher to always be conscious in every activity they perform in the presence of the children. The teacher must work at the most ordinary of tasks humbly, artistically and joyfully. The teacher must think about and sacrifice themselves, disciplining those human activities of breathing, sleeping and waking, moving and speaking to be worthy of the imitation of the child who beholds them in the classroom.

Through their work with young children, early childhood educators have a tremendous opportunity for active self development. Steiner describes this opportunity in the following way:

> Spiritual science is something that acts according to the model of a being encompassing a higher Self, just as we embrace other beings in sympathy with their sorrows and joys without losing ourselves. When we know our expanded selves with which we penetrate to other individual beings, then we can speak about children in the following way: Besides what we take hold of as educators developing out of our normal consciousness, something is already working on the child as a higher being outside of his normal self. If we focus on this, we will perhaps find another kind of education at work on the child, whereas in our normal education we turn only to the personal self of the child. (Steiner, 1995, p.10)

The curriculum in a Waldorf early childhood classroom evolves around the development of the will through the activities of movement, speech and gesture, play and work. The youngest child in the class has the freedom to move and each individual child's initial experience of play is honored and protected. The middle kindergartner explores and imitates whatever is in the environment through fantasy play. The older kindergartner develops ideas through social play balanced in rhythm with the artistic, practical and meaningful work of kindergarten. When we make space for free play, we are honoring and revering the highest human quality. Steiner speaks of play as being that which works on the child as a higher self.

It is children's play, the meaningful, well carried out play of all children, that the higher Self works on. With the child's play we can only create preconditions for an education. What is accomplished in play happens basically through the self-activity of the child, through everything that cannot be confined to strict rules. Indeed, the essential, educational aspect of play is based on the fact that we call a halt to our rules and to all our arts of education and leave the child to his own impulses. For what does a child do when we leave him to his own impulses? When playing with external objects the child can try out whether this or that will work through his...activity. He brings his own will into activity, into movement. Because of the way in which the external objects behave under the influence of the will, it then happens that the child educates himself for life, simply through play. ... The more that play has to do with what cannot be comprehended but is simply beheld in its living character, the better it is. (Steiner, 1995, p.11)

The Child's First Experience of School

When is a child really born? A sensitive parent will tell you that a child is known long before conception. What a parent shares with a teacher about their child before they are born into school is special and very important to developing the relationship the child has to school. The interest and manner in which that first teacher receives that information can be invaluable to all teachers who follow. What do we really need to know in the beginning and all along the way? What are the questions we need to ask at each developmental point? What are the chapters in this book called "human being"?

In the beginning, it is important to listen to what the parent wants to share. It is important to honor the relationship that the parent and child have and understand the change that is about to take place. "Tell me about your child" is the first question at the first conference between teacher and parents. As the parent shares the details of the child's first years of life, it is important to listen to each detail as if it were a facet of a precious crystal, for to a parent, this short time they have shared with this child is entirely life transforming. It is important not to criticize even inwardly how they have parented their child. It is important to try to listen without taking notes and write down the impressions later upon reflection. Write the story as you remember it. Kindergarten teachers can have parents write their special memories as part of the birthday celebration, but from the initial interview, it is best that the teacher reflect upon what has been said and how the parent said it. It is good to 'sleep on it' and write impressions the next morning. There will be ample time for concrete observations, but an impression of this first interview will guide you tenderly into a relationship with the environment the child has shared called 'family'. It is even important to have this interview before the first home visit, because the interview will offer clues for entering into the environment where this family has grown together.

Working with Parents

Teachers are required to be 'trained' these days. We go to school, study hard and walk away from that concentrated time thinking we know everything there is to know about the subject of teaching children. In fact we only 'know' theory, and this includes teachers who have participated in Waldorf trainings. Those of us who have not been parents need to delete the words 'should' and 'must' from our vocabulary and not offer criticism before they have experienced some practical time teaching children and sharing those children with

their parents. Even then, providing parents with ideas and solutions rather than criticisms and rules, will be a more productive means of interacting. Nursery teachers must particularly keep in mind that they are the beginning of the social environment called school. Many parents are very tentative about sharing their child with the school. School changes everything. In some ways theses changes are good, in other ways they are perceived as much less positive. Some parents never choose to share their children so we must be always grateful for the choice parents make to share their child with us. We need to meet the parents with humility and gratitude.

It is important to enter into this relationship with parents and child with the deepest reverence. Certainly you will meet parents who will have made the greatest mistakes possible according to your training, but the fact is that this child chose these parents. This child is also choosing his first teacher to guide the family into the environment of school. The nursery teacher must understand that parents are intimately involved in the growth and life of the child and whatever occurs in the environment of family has to do with family karma that must be recognized with a certain acceptance from teachers. Nursery teachers must receive the family in 'flowing sensitivity'; our soul formation must be neutral and "balanced between sympathy and antipathy." We must be "constantly receptive to impressions" and "show a relationship to much of what comes to meet" our soul. (Steiner, 1994, p.105)

The Teacher's Inner Work

So we have had the first interview and then reflect on the interview in our meditative life. Before going to bed, first imagine "the angel who stands behind you as an individual gently laying hands upon your head." Then imagine above your angel a circle of Archangels who are deeply interested in the task of teaching human beings. Then imagine a point which is the Archai who are interested in the evolution of mankind. (Steiner, 1996a, p.46) Then bring to mind the interview you shared with the child's parents; recall everything you are able to remember. "What human beings receive from the higher worlds comes to them during sleep." (Steiner, 1996a, p.42) In the morning, when you have the impulse, write down what you can of this first interview. Remember to write it down with awareness that everything written is something concrete in the world. This is the first paragraph in the first chapter in the child's book of school life.

Home Visit

The second phase is the home visit, and once again it is good to go through the same process as with the first interview. Enter the child's home with reverence and gratitude and bring your impressions into your sleep, for we are continuing the process the angels started before birth, and they have much to tell us. "We want to be aware that physical existence is a continuance of the spiritual life. What we have to do in education is a continuation of what higher beings have done without our assistance." (Steiner, 1996a, p.37)

First Day of School

Now we are at the first day of school. We have had our first interviews and our home visits. We have carefully prepared our classrooms, polishing all of the wooden toys, ironing the silks, memorizing our circle and preparing ingredients for bread. We have invited the angels to participate. The door opens and as we greet the children we receive new impressions. How does the social organism of 'class' come together and what is it that each child brings to that organism? In a way, on that first day of school, we enter the ring of the Archangels. And this becomes the third paragraph in the child's first year of school.

These precious first three paragraphs are perceptions of the threshold. Children guide us in an immediate way to the threshold and we can learn so much about their relationship to the threshold by sharing this time with them consciously. We need to ask questions of the parents and we need to observe and ask questions within

ourselves. The developing human being has many different sides and although it is important how we record and process what we observe, it is also important that we as kindergarten teachers find a way to convey the unfolding story of the early development of each child. This story will unlock many doors and guide us to avenues that will help the child engage in the very human experience of breathing into life.

As we begin to engage in observation, it is best to try to see the child's relationship to the environment. How does the child enter the room? If the child has been through some sort of bridging program at the school, separation is probably not a problem. However, each classroom experience presents a new picture of 'school' for the child. In the first three weeks of school, it is good to observe each child, perhaps two each day, being open to impressions that come and recording observations: Are the children separating from their parents? How does each child enter the classroom? Does the child seem happy or sad, angry or glad? Does the child get ready for school or sit on the bench waiting for help? Does the child become involved with other children or hang back? What role does the child take up in the school environment? Does the child observe, charge into play or want to help the teacher? When you have made these observations and recorded them, you have a picture of how the child related to school in the beginning and you have something to tell the parents in the first formal school conference.

Parent conferences are vital in the first year. It would be good to have scheduled quarterly conferences the first year and be open to requests for additional conferences from parents. (This is a requirement for early childhood teachers who are teaching nursery-age children.) If parents are met frequently in the first year, then conferences from the second year on can be fewer and are more efficient. The first conferences also provide a base-line of information for the teacher about the child that only the parents hold. There are many questions that need to be asked, and it is best to ask them over a stretch of several conferences rather than assuming you can hear everything about the first three years of the child's life in the first conference This information should come to the teacher through conversation rather than a questionnaire. The relationship to school is a new one for the parent as much as it is to the nursery child. Each child is different and even if the family is presenting you with their third child, how that child relates to the school can be an entirely different picture from the first or second child.

The first conference after school begins could be a sharing of how the child is doing in school. If you have recorded your observations in writing, not only will you have a beginning picture for the school, but you can share a true picture of each child with the parents. Just as you have observed the children, it is also good to keep a conference log, writing your impression of the meeting you had with the parents, noting their reactions and concerns, which can also be a stepping off place for the next conference. (See an example of a "Conference Log" at the end of this section).

It is a good idea to separate each conference thematically, asking questions about different aspects of the child's beginning. For example, pregnancy, birth and early development questions could

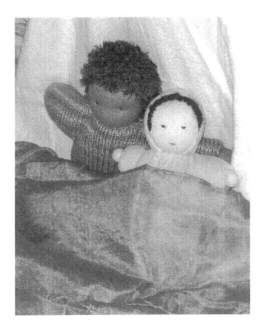

be covered in the first conference. The second conference might attend to the child's relationship to eating and sleeping which relates more to the initial social experience of the child. Most schools require parents to fill out a health form and certainly the teacher should read the form and discuss questions of medical needs that might impact the child in the classroom at the first, not the second conference. But basically, our questions to the parents open the door for a narrative picture of the child's beginning development. (See "Conference Questions for Parents" at the end of this section.)

New families are often independent from their extended family. Some young parents are close to their families and others may have many ideas about parenting that are reactive. That is, they parent exactly the opposite of the parenting style of their own parents. The prevailing view of these phenomena is that most parents have lost their instincts for parenting. Actually, they have lost their generational continuity. In earlier times, human beings learned to parent from their own parents. On the whole, we have become independent or estranged from generational ties. Keeping this in mind, it is probably not the best course of action to meet the parents of the children we are teaching with the assumption that they are learners needing to be taught the "users manual" for their child. When talking about parenting style, we can pose the questions and listen to what the parents share without much comment or judgment. Information about healthy parenting can be imparted topically during general parent meetings and lectures. If this information is attended to in a more general manner, it will be more likely to have an impact and the whole school community will be aware that the topics have been broached.

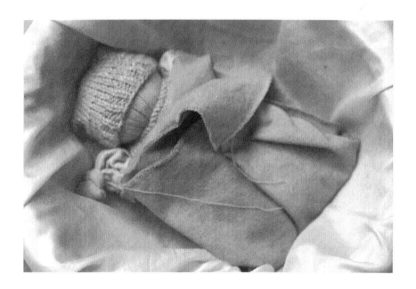

Conference Log

Teacher: C. Lang
Class: Nursery Class

Date:	Observation or Outcome
9/7 10AM	Home visit Alyssa Shares bedroom w/brother (1)
9/7 6PM	Home visit Kristin Only child/large master bedroom
9/10 11AM	Home visit Adam Only child, TV in bedroom
9/10 2PM	Home visit Ben Macrobiotic family/warm home
9/11 9AM	Home visit Alexander Two homes/2 complete bedrooms
9/11 10AM	Home visit Casey Empty playroom draw on walls
9/11 11AM	Tea with returning children Jessica chatty — out of shell
9/11 1PM	Home visit with Halley All family there/small apt.
9/13 2PM	Home visit with Arielle Only child/Mom works at home
9/18 6PM	Food issue meeting – Three parents and Kindergarten teacher were present to discuss individual and general food issues. Issues will be brought to the preschool faculty meeting to determine resolutions.
9/18 7PM	New Parents' Meeting
9/20 7PM	Conference with Emily's parents, who are concerned that their child is so much bigger than the other children. They thought perhaps she

belongs in the kindergarten. Emily's social behavior and inability to dress herself or complete any task independently suggest that she is in the right class.

10/2 7PM Class meeting – 100% class parent turnout, discussion of classroom rhythm and how to support it at home.

10/11 6PM Conference with Kirsten's parents discussing mother's terminal illness and how to help child

10/12 AM Adam sits in W and seems to have balance problems

10/12 6PM Phoned Adam's mom to discuss observations – she is willing to work with me doing movement exercises at home – gave permission that I could share my observations in the care group

Conference Questions for Parents

Name of Child: Date of Birth:
Pregnancy and Birth:
Mother: Father:

What is the birth order of the child?
Were you trying to have a baby or was this child a bit of a
    surprise?
At what point in the pregnancy did you become aware that
    you were pregnant?
What was it like when you found out you were pregnant?
What qualities distinguished your pregnancy? Did you have
    morning sickness? Did you have a lot of energy?
Did you work throughout your pregnancy?
What type of work did you do?
At what point in the pregnancy did you stop working?
Did you exercise throughout your pregnancy? If you exercised
what type of exercise did you do?
Did you crave foods during your pregnancy?
Did you have traditional pre-natal care or did you go to a
    midwife?
Did you and your husband/partner go to prenatal classes?
Did your pregnancy go to term?
Was the baby born in the hospital, midwife in the hospital or
    home birth?
Who was present at the birth of your child?
Would you share the story of your child's birth?
Did you nurse or was the baby bottle-fed?
Would you share your experience feeding your child?
Did you have any difficulty with post-partum depression?
What was it like developing a rhythm for your baby?
Did you have a non-family member child caregiver directly
    after birth or did you have family help?
Would you describe the situation you had in the beginning?

OBSERVATION AND ASSESSMENT

The Nursery Child

Typically assessment is something that the school or teacher requests from other professionals. However, it is important that teachers know what to look for to determine when outside intervention is an appropriate necessity. Often the child's teacher is the initiator of outside assessment. Is it always necessary to reach outside the classroom? Is it possible to develop a process to determine the individual needs of the children, work within the classroom to make adaptations and meet those needs and allow the child to grow and possibly work through the perceived difficulties?

When it comes to assessment during the preschool years, we have tools available as teachers. We have are our ability to observe with our senses the visible phenomena and then bring what we observe and our questions before our meditative eye or into our thinking. Young children present many questions and often express something quite opposite to that which we would expect from our adult experience and perspective. We can guide our observations toward three areas: the form (thinking); the way the child relates to the world through his lower senses (touch, life, self-movement and balance) and begins to be involved in a social experience (feeling); and the organizational development of the body or how the child is growing (willing).

Looking into the nursery at the youngest children entering the kindergarten, our attention is drawn to their form and movement. The social life is in still in seed form. The three- to four-year-old has a form that is round and the head is emphasized or larger than the rest of the body. If you juxtapose this against the oldest children in the Kindergarten, age six to six and a half, you can see they have obtained a three-folding of their physical form and appear relatively differentiated (head, torso and limbs) and balanced. This differentiation and balance should also be apparent in social and physical capacities, as well as the child's approach to the world which should be reasonably well developed at this stage.

The physical form of the youngest children seems to be mostly head. Their bodies, torso and limbs seem to be growing out of their head and their limbs and bodies are typically soft, round and undifferentiated. The second impression we often have is that socially they are isolated in their own little world and if they make contact with someone other than their parents, it is a shock or a surprise or forever a new experience. (Lievegoed, 1985) Finally, when we observe their limbs, we notice that, upon achieving uprightness and movement, they immediately try to imitate the speed of the adults in the environment and they run, grab and bump in a clumsy and inaccurate manner. It is almost as if they reach stability through chaos. What mother doesn't know how frustrating it is when her child begins to explore the environment in earnest?

We now have before us in the two and a half year old, the almost-school-age child, a threefold human being with an emphasis upon the head, a rudimentary interest in others and a primitive capacity to explore the world. Do we then rip the child out of that beginning exploration and do an assessment? No, in a Waldorf early childhood program, the next four years are about the environment adapting and changing to suit the needs of the growing child rather than the child adapting to the environment. If there needs to be accommodation then, it needs to be through the parent outside of the classroom or the teacher within the classroom.

One could well point out that there are many young children these days who are going for outside assessments, or put in occupational therapy or even play therapy. Although there is nothing really wrong with therapy and certainly there are situations that require it, of what use is it to place a child in an OT gym twice a week and not incorporate the therapeutic movement or sensory diet into the child's environment and daily rhythm?

What is good for one child is likely good for all the children, but it is entirely certain that the social environment of family and classroom is more useful towards integration into the world than isolation or separation. Individual therapies can often segregate the child who then senses he is different from his peers. Differences are indeed part of life experience but should not isolate. It should not be the first conclusion we come to that there is something wrong with the child. We adults, teachers and parents, need to help the young child enter into the world through observation and questioning, then adaptation of the environment and personal work. The children whom I have met who truly are ill or disabled strive to get better and we should honor and be honored by the fact that they want to be part of our world.

One way to begin to develop a process for observation, assessment and intervention, is to determine different areas and criteria of observation guided by the growth and development of the children. When observing the three- to three-and-a-half-year-old, our observations should be guided by the child's form: whether he is developing in the lower senses and if there appear to be difficulties with movement, balance, or touch, and whether the child has gone through and overcome developmental milestones at the appropriate time and in the appropriate sequence. When observing the middle kindergartner, age four to five, beginning social engagement, visible growth and development of the body, and a clear interest in kindergarten activities will guide our observations. Finally, the oldest kindergartner, age five to six or six-and-a-half by the end of the school year, will have a stretched, lengthened and differentiated form, a real capacity for work or play, developed speech, an ability for imaginative and sequential thinking, and a sense of belonging to the class.

Of course it is not enough just to observe; our observations bring up questions or riddles for which the answers will be what is needed to help the child continue to grow and develop. These questions can be brought into our sleep, faculty or early childhood meetings, or to the care group if one exists. Sharing the child with others and desiring to understand the child are the first steps towards taking action. Action involves adaptations of the classroom, or transformations of our thinking, or interaction with the community, all on behalf of the child.

One of the greatest hindrances to young children is the retention of early movement patterns or the developmental reflexes. These movement patterns are naturally overcome in sequential order and should certainly be entirely inhibited by the time the child enters preschool. Thanks to Peter Blythe and Sally Goddard, we have easily observable symptoms that point to retention of early movement patterns. If these symptoms do exist, incorporation of early movement patterns such as rolling, creeping, crawling, balancing, etc. can be emphasized in playtime, work, or crafts. (See the "Guidelines for the Observation of Retained Early Movement Patterns" at the end of this section. This report can also be an individual record of observation for file keeping.)

These observations can be taken up generally or individually, but it is good to become familiar enough with the symptoms that might suggest retained early movement patterns so that classroom intervention can take place. Opportunities for all kinds of developmental movement practice are important to incorporate in all nursery classrooms. When observing the children it is good to record observations both initially and, if symptoms are present, to regularly observe if general intervention has enabled the child to overcome these immature movement patterns. Observation coupled with conferences with parents can lead to a deeper understanding of why the child has retained these movement patterns. If the reflexes have not been observably overcome by the end of the nursery year, the child may need more practice or a deeper intervention. This could be left until the beginning of the middle kindergarten year. How further intervention is determined is beyond the scope of this book, but the first step might be to bring the child to the faculty or care group. If there is a school doctor, a curative eurythmist or an extra lesson teacher, an individual plan could be developed and incorporated into the school day.

Guidelines for Observation:
Retained Early Movement Patterns Report

Name of Child:
Date of Birth:
Teacher: Today's Date:

Observable symptoms suggestive of retained reflex from higher order to lower in a kindergarten-age child:

Symmetrical Tonic Neck Reflex (STNR)
This reflex emerges 6–9 months, inhibited 9–11 months. It helps the baby overcome gravity by getting up off the floor on to hands and knees. This reflex is not in primitive category or the postural category. It could be called a transitional reflex. Flexion of the head on the forehead against the floor causes infant to bend arms and extend legs. Extension of the head in the upright position causes infant to bend legs and the straighten arms creating a 'crawling-ready' posture.

Symptom	Present	Not Present
Poor posture	☐	☐
Tendency to slump in chair	☐	☐
Tendency to lay head on table	☐	☐
Simian (ape-like) walk	☐	☐
'W' leg position when sitting on the floor	☐	☐
Messy eater	☐	☐
Clumsy – drops and spills	☐	☐
Unable to imitate	☐	☐
Unable to catch or throw a ball	☐	☐

Tonic Labyrinthine Reflex (TLR)
This reflex is vestibular in origin. Forward reflex emerges *in utero,* inhibited 4 months – fetal position. Backward reflex emerges at birth when head enters the birth canal and is inhibited gradually from 6 months to 3 years (helps infant to overcome fetal positioning). It is related closely to the Moro reflex and influences muscle tone throughout the body. This reflex has an impact on the control of the head in an upright position, balance and movement forward and back.

Symptom	Present	Not Present
Posture – stoops/looks at the ground (forward)	☐	☐
Posture – tendency to walk on toes (backward)	☐	☐
Weak muscle tone (forward)	☐	☐
Stiff and jerky movements (backward)	☐	☐
Poor sense of balance	☐	☐
Poor sense of coordination (backward)	☐	☐
Tendency to motion sickness (gets carsick)	☐	☐
Doesn't like to move quickly (forward)	☐	☐
Bumps into things	☐	☐

Spinal Galant
This reflex emerges 20 weeks *in utero*, is actively present at birth and inhibited 3–9 months of life. When the infant is lying face down, brushing ones finger along one side of the spine will cause the child to flex and rotate hip on the side of the stimulus. Present on both sides. May help move the fetus down the birth canal.

Symptom	Present	Not Present
Fidgeting (ants-in-pants syndrome)	☐	☐
Poor concentration	☐	☐
Inability to retain classroom rhythm	☐	☐
Hip rotation to one side when walking	☐	☐
Toileting accidents	☐	☐
Bedwetting	☐	☐

Asymmetrical Tonic Neck Reflex (ATNR)
This reflex emerges 18 weeks *in utero*, is actively present at birth and inhibited at 6 months of life. Movement of head to one side will cause the infant to extend the arm and leg on the side the head is turned to, and flex the arm and leg on the opposite side. This reflex assists in continuous motion *in utero*, positioning the fetus when it moves down birth canal and the birth process reinforces the reflex. It also develops muscle tone and provides balance (vestibular) stimulation. After birth ATNR stimulates eye-hand coordination and higher order skills leading to crawling and uprightness and balance for walking. C-section babies may show many symptoms because it is stimulated during the birth process

Symptom	Present	Not Present
Balance affected by head movement	☐	☐
Difficulty with cross-pattern movement	☐	☐
Difficulty crossing the midline	☐	☐
Mixed laterality	☐	☐

Palmar Reflex
This reflex emerges around 11 weeks *in utero*, is fully present at birth, and is inhibited at 2–3 months of life. It develops the capacity to grasp and release, refines finger control and is replaced by pincer grip at 36 weeks of age.

Symptom	Present	Not Present
Poor manual dexterity	☐	☐
Lack of independent thumb and finger movement (cannot shake hands)	☐	☐
Palm of hand hypersensitive	☐	☐
Child moves mouth when trying to write/draw	☐	☐

Moro Reflex
This reflex emerges 9 weeks *in utero*, is fully present at birth and is inhibited at 2–4 months of life. An involuntary reaction to threat causes the infant to startle and move limbs in an outward reaction, then clasp arms to body.

Symptom	Present	Not Present
Poor balance	☐	☐
Physical timidity	☐	☐
Visual confusion/sensitivity (overwhelmed)	☐	☐
Auditory confusion/sensitivity (overwhelmed)	☐	☐
Overwhelmed and reacts to smells	☐	☐
Cannot go from general to specific	☐	☐
Allergies	☐	☐
Dislikes and reacts to change	☐	☐
Holds breath	☐	☐
Hyperventilates	☐	☐
Insecure and dependent	☐	☐

The Middle Kindergartner

The four- to five-year-old child represents the heart of the early childhood program. Children of this age are ready to meet the curriculum provided in a Waldorf setting. Since not all children are equally ready to be in kindergarten, and that includes children who have come from Waldorf parent/child, bridging or even nursery programs, it is important to look at what a kindergarten-ready child looks like.

Physically, the healthy kindergarten-ready children have lost the unity of roundness and have developed limbs. Their form is still soft, but there is a distinct lengthening of their limbs. Their gaze is often still cosmic, but one has the sense that they, unlike the three-year-old, observe the adult even though they do not meet the gaze of the adult. They seem to defy gravity when they run, jump and generally move. They can be independent from their parent. A middle kindergarten child is usually comfortable and can adapt to the environment of the kindergarten if it is a safe environment which is well thought out to meet the needs of the young child. They can sustain a morning program of four hours without a nap or long rest. They can go to the bathroom and dress themselves. They should be sturdy and healthy with a robust or rosy coloring and they should not be susceptible to frequent illness. (Almon, 1988)

The initial impression one should have of children who are entering the middle kindergarten phase of school is that they have reached a certain level of independence and are now ready to for social play and work. This social engagement through play and work tends to be the main focus of the curriculum in the middle kindergarten. A child's social capacities are often the focus of our observations and interventions during this middle kindergarten year even if the children are in a mixed-age kindergarten. The blessing of the mixed age kindergarten is that the children of all age groups have available exposure to multi-level opportunities for movement, skill development, and social and language development. So while the middle kindergartner is mainly practicing at work and play, he can also observe and take part in tasks and activities that the older kindergartner is ready for. A mixed-age kindergarten is a wonderfully rich environment for the development of the senses and offers many opportunities for observation and imitation.

When the children begin the middle kindergarten school year, during the first month the teacher's observations should be directed again at the early movement patterns. There will be new children entering the school who will need assessment. There will be children who raised questions at the end of the nursery school year who may need further intervention or who may have overcome these patterns during school break. These initial assessments will be useful for targeting individual needs and developing and incorporating movement opportunities in the classroom. If the children have not overcome these early patterns, activities that require more complex movement will be challenging if not impossible. Some behaviors can also be alleviated by working to overcome these patterns. Finally, if these early movement patterns remain into the middle year of kindergarten, the child may need more intervention than can be provided in the classroom. There are many therapies available. Outside intervention can include cranial sacral work, rhythmic massage, curative eurythmy or anthroposophical medicine. Once movement needs have been addressed, the transition into healthy play and work will be smoother and more fruitful.

The middle kindergartner continues to be both a sense being and a will being. What this means is that everything within the environment of the child will be taken into the physical body through imitation and the child will incorporate what he experiences in the outer world into his physical body and his organs. However, since the middle kindergartner has taken on a bit more form, as defined by the lengthening of the limbs, and if the child is generally healthy and the environment is healthy, then the child can begin to be more selective.

Between the fourth and fifth years there is a notable transition in the children's play. As the children begin this year at the age of four, their play becomes fantasy oriented. Objects become an impulse for play and can even suggest play — a stone can become a potato which the child cooks over an open fire or it can become a baby cradled in the child's arms. This imaginative play and the impulse to imitate guide the child into fledgling social interactions. The curriculum of the classroom, story telling, the songs and games of the circle, the kindergarten work and the play of the older children also guide the four- to five-year-old, through the impulse to imitate, to acquire new skills for play through language acquisition, problem solving and developed physical skillfulness.

A checklist can be used to develop a process of observations of the middle kindergartner. (See the "Middle Kindergarten Checklist" at the end of this section.) This checklist is meant to be a guide for the teacher offering a middle kindergarten picture of the child. The reflexes might be observed in the beginning of the school year, and the list checked again as the child nears the fifth birthday. However, the intention is to also provide a means of observation relative to the middle kindergartner that could support conferences with the parents which will be less frequent than in the nursery classroom year. These observations are also intended to provide a picture of the health of the child and the health of the classroom, as well as year-end report writing.

Middle Kindergarten Checklist

Name of Child: _____ Date of Birth: _____
Teacher: _____ Date of Assessment: _____

Category	Immature	Progressing	Mature	Concern	N/A
PHYSICAL DEVELOPMENT					
Head to body ratio 1:5	☐	☐	☐	☐	☐
Lengthening of limbs	☐	☐	☐	☐	☐
Knees visible	☐	☐	☐	☐	☐
Collarbone visible	☐	☐	☐	☐	☐
Visible musculature in legs	☐	☐	☐	☐	☐
Beginning waist incision	☐	☐	☐	☐	☐
Abdomen flattens	☐	☐	☐	☐	☐
Beginning S curve in spine	☐	☐	☐	☐	☐
MOVEMENT					
Walking	☐	☐	☐	☐	☐
Running	☐	☐	☐	☐	☐
Galloping	☐	☐	☐	☐	☐
Skipping	☐	☐	☐	☐	☐
Jumping	☐	☐	☐	☐	☐
Hopping (2)	☐	☐	☐	☐	☐
Hopping (1)	☐	☐	☐	☐	☐

Category	Immature	Progressing	Mature	Concern	N/A
BALANCE					
Stand with both feet together	☐	☐	☐	☐	☐
Stand on one foot	☐	☐	☐	☐	☐
Can walk in a line	☐	☐	☐	☐	☐
Can walk without touching anything	☐	☐	☐	☐	☐
LANGUAGE DEVELOPMENT					
Imitates language heard in environment during play	☐	☐	☐	☐	☐
Imitates gesture during circle	☐	☐	☐	☐	☐
Immersed during story and circle time	☐	☐	☐	☐	☐
Can articulate needs	☐	☐	☐	☐	☐
PLAY AND IMAGINATION					
Fantasy based	☐	☐	☐	☐	☐
Begins to incorporate others	☐	☐	☐	☐	☐
Immersed in imagination throughout morning	☐	☐	☐	☐	☐
Can be redirected imaginatively	☐	☐	☐	☐	☐

Category	Immature	Progressing	Mature	Concern	N/A
ARTISTIC					
Paints and colors without form	☐	☐	☐	☐	☐
Incorporates color into play	☐	☐	☐	☐	☐
Incorporates craft activities into play themes	☐	☐	☐	☐	☐
Can warm and sculpt beeswax	☐	☐	☐	☐	☐
INDEPENDENCE AND TRANSITIONS					
Can move with the class during transitions	☐	☐	☐	☐	☐
Can incorporate change without reacting	☐	☐	☐	☐	☐
Can dress self	☐	☐	☐	☐	☐
Can take care of bathroom needs independently	☐	☐	☐	☐	☐
Can get ready to go home	☐	☐	☐	☐	☐
Can wait patiently	☐	☐	☐	☐	☐

The Older Kindergarten Child

The older kindergarten child, ages five to six, is actively preparing for school. The older child usually begins the final kindergarten year immersed in fantasy play but is aware of the children who were his playmates at the end of the previous school year. It is now that true friendships begin. The children are happy to be together again. They band together and begin to repeat themes for play or challenges to be met. As the year passes their play moves out of fantasy, and they spend time developing ideas for play. The stone no longer takes on imaginative characteristics, but becomes a means for building a dam or forming the foundation of a house, or whatever idea they want to build.

The older child often goes through a midyear crisis with play and needs to be met with work and opportunities to develop fine motor skills through crafts. This is an important time for the kindergarten child, and one could say a question of elementary school ripeness looms large if the child does not stop and work at becoming a student. As the initial crisis passes, a balance of work and play now needs to be provided throughout the remainder of the final kindergarten year.

The transition from the kindergarten to the elementary school is one that needs to be carefully observed and documented. Although the kindergarten and the elementary school represent different aspects of child development, it is important that the first grade teacher, who in a Waldorf school will follow the children for eight years, has a picture of the early development of each child in the class. All too often there is little communication between the kindergarten and the elementary school. However, a process for observation in the kindergarten from the beginning of school entrance until the transition into the first grade offers a starting place for community interaction.

The process during the school year for kindergarten transition observations could include a team made up of the kindergarten faculty, an extra lesson/special education teacher, the doctor, the curative eurythmist and an experienced first grade teacher who represents the teacher of the rising first grade if that teacher cannot be present or is a first-time class teacher.

The Transitional Kindergarten Report is intended for the child of six who is showing signs of moving toward elementary school ripeness. It can be divided into sections which outside observers can perform for the teacher. Some sections require the observation of the kindergarten teachers who spend time daily with the children. (See the "Transitional Kindergarten Report" at the end of this section.)

The year-end Kindergarten Assessment is intended for those children who are being considered for first grade. (See the Kindergarten Assessment Checklist and the Kindergarten Assessment Story at the end of this section.) Using this checklist and the information compiled over the kindergarten years, the faculty can meet and discuss the readiness of students for admission to first grade. If a process has evolved over the kindergarten years, there should be clarity of any delays long before the middle or end of the final kindergarten year. Each school can develop its own way of meeting to discuss first grade readiness. However if a process of observation has been maintained and reviewed throughout the kindergarten years, a clear and developing picture of individual children should evolve.

The Kindergarten Assessment is the culminating picture of the kindergarten child and creates a baseline or first picture of the elementary school child. Some aspects of child development should be in place long before the child enters first grade. As an example, if the early movement patterns have not been inhibited, becoming aware of this during the second grade assessment is far too late for the child's healthy development and success as a student.

Kindergarten Transition Report

Name of Child: _____ Date of Birth: _____

Teacher: _____ Date of Assessment: _____

Category	Immature	Progressing	Mature	Concern	N/A
PHYSICAL CHARACTERISTICS					
Head-to-body ratio (age 7 - 1:6)	☐	☐	☐	☐	☐
Three-folding of body (head-trunk-limbs)	☐	☐	☐	☐	☐
Neck incision	☐	☐	☐	☐	☐
Waist incision	☐	☐	☐	☐	☐
Lengthening of limbs	☐	☐	☐	☐	☐
Touch top of ear w/arm over head	☐	☐	☐	☐	☐
Visible joints (knuckles and kneecaps)	☐	☐	☐	☐	☐
Beginning of visible musculature	☐	☐	☐	☐	☐
Visible arch in foot	☐	☐	☐	☐	☐
S curve in back	☐	☐	☐	☐	☐
Second dentition (number of teeth)	☐	☐	☐	☐	☐
Individualized facial features	☐	☐	☐	☐	☐
Gaze direct and eye to eye	☐	☐	☐	☐	☐
SPEECH AND LANGUAGE					
Clarity and enunciation	☐	☐	☐	☐	☐
Speaks in complete sentences	☐	☐	☐	☐	☐
Expresses ideas clearly and fully	☐	☐	☐	☐	☐
Uses if/therefore (cause/effect)	☐	☐	☐	☐	☐

Category	Immature	Progressing	Mature	Concern	N/A
Talks about play (visualization)	☐	☐	☐	☐	☐
Enjoys rhymes and limericks	☐	☐	☐	☐	☐
Can tell a story	☐	☐	☐	☐	☐
Observable physical abilities	☐	☐	☐	☐	☐

FOUR LOWER SENSES

Sense of Balance:

Stand with both feet together	☐	☐	☐	☐	☐
Stand on one foot	☐	☐	☐	☐	☐
Can walk in a line	☐	☐	☐	☐	☐
Can walk w/out touching anything	☐	☐	☐	☐	☐

Sense of Movement:

Walks cross laterally	☐	☐	☐	☐	☐
Marches cross laterally	☐	☐	☐	☐	☐
Runs cross laterally	☐	☐	☐	☐	☐
Hops on either foot	☐	☐	☐	☐	☐
Bunny hop (both feet together)	☐	☐	☐	☐	☐
Walks backward	☐	☐	☐	☐	☐
Gallops	☐	☐	☐	☐	☐
Skips	☐	☐	☐	☐	☐
Climbs stairs alternating feet	☐	☐	☐	☐	☐
Runs with a fluidity of gait	☐	☐	☐	☐	☐
Makes transitions easily	☐	☐	☐	☐	☐
Accepts changes	☐	☐	☐	☐	☐
Reacts well to new experience	☐	☐	☐	☐	☐

Category	Immature	Progressing	Mature	Concern	N/A
Sense of Life:					
Always at school	☐	☐	☐	☐	☐
Healthy rosy coloring	☐	☐	☐	☐	☐
Warm hands	☐	☐	☐	☐	☐
Wet hands	☐	☐	☐	☐	☐
Falls asleep easily	☐	☐	☐	☐	☐
Breaths normally	☐	☐	☐	☐	☐
Stamina/endurance	☐	☐	☐	☐	☐
Is a harmonious member of class	☐	☐	☐	☐	☐
Participates in activities happily	☐	☐	☐	☐	☐
Eats food made in the classroom	☐	☐	☐	☐	☐
Has friends in the classroom	☐	☐	☐	☐	☐
Has positive relationships with adults	☐	☐	☐	☐	☐
Has a sense of humor	☐	☐	☐	☐	☐
Can look after personal needs	☐	☐	☐	☐	☐
Is comfortable alone	☐	☐	☐	☐	☐
Sense of privacy (tells secrets)	☐	☐	☐	☐	☐
Sense of Touch:					
Can imitate	☐	☐	☐	☐	☐
Has a sense of body in space	☐	☐	☐	☐	☐
Can follow directions (group)	☐	☐	☐	☐	☐
Can follow directions (individual)	☐	☐	☐	☐	☐
Completes activities independently	☐	☐	☐	☐	☐
Experiences limits and boundaries	☐	☐	☐	☐	☐

Category	Immature	Progressing	Mature	Concern	N/A
Has compassion for others	☐	☐	☐	☐	☐
Tells a story in sequence	☐	☐	☐	☐	☐
Observable Capacities:					
Shoes on correct feet	☐	☐	☐	☐	☐
Kempt and tidy	☐	☐	☐	☐	☐
Hair brushed/combed	☐	☐	☐	☐	☐
Can tie shoes successfully	☐	☐	☐	☐	☐
Zips successfully	☐	☐	☐	☐	☐
Buttons successfully and sequentially	☐	☐	☐	☐	☐
Visible bruises/scars	☐	☐	☐	☐	☐
Can catch a ball	☐	☐	☐	☐	☐
Can throw a ball	☐	☐	☐	☐	☐
Can unpack or pack independently	☐	☐	☐	☐	☐
Can draw with details	☐	☐	☐	☐	☐
Can sew a running stitch	☐	☐	☐	☐	☐
Can finger knit	☐	☐	☐	☐	☐
Can retell a story	☐	☐	☐	☐	☐
Shakes hands thumb in opposition	☐	☐	☐	☐	☐
Participation in the curriculum	☐	☐	☐	☐	☐
Recognizes consequences	☐	☐	☐	☐	☐
Internalization of classroom routine	☐	☐	☐	☐	☐
Respect for property of others	☐	☐	☐	☐	☐
Respect for personal property	☐	☐	☐	☐	☐
Has the ability to share	☐	☐	☐	☐	☐
Morning circle:					
Enters into activity willingly	☐	☐	☐	☐	☐
Participates in activity	☐	☐	☐	☐	☐

Category	Immature	Progressing	Mature	Concern	N/A
Play:					
Seeks out friends for play	☐	☐	☐	☐	☐
Includes children not within circle of friends in play	☐	☐	☐	☐	☐
Can share					
Can plan and negotiate play	☐	☐	☐	☐	☐
Develops imaginative stories for play	☐	☐	☐	☐	☐
Can continue a story into next day	☐	☐	☐	☐	☐
Has a sense for the dramatic	☐	☐	☐	☐	☐
Has a sense for what is humorous	☐	☐	☐	☐	☐
Clean-up:					
Enters into the activity willingly	☐	☐	☐	☐	☐
Knows what needs to be done	☐	☐	☐	☐	☐
Can give a task full attention	☐	☐	☐	☐	☐
Can follow through multiple steps	☐	☐	☐	☐	☐
Has the ability to complete a task	☐	☐	☐	☐	☐
Can follow instructions if given	☐	☐	☐	☐	☐
Baking:					
Enters into activity willingly	☐	☐	☐	☐	☐
Participates in activity	☐	☐	☐	☐	☐
Can remain focused during activity	☐	☐	☐	☐	☐
Can complete activity with class	☐	☐	☐	☐	☐

Category	Immature	Progressing	Mature	Concern	N/A
Crafts:					
Enters into activity willingly	☐	☐	☐	☐	☐
Participates in activity	☐	☐	☐	☐	☐
Can observe and follow directions	☐	☐	☐	☐	☐
Can remain focused during activity	☐	☐	☐	☐	☐
Can ask for help	☐	☐	☐	☐	☐
Can complete craft independently	☐	☐	☐	☐	☐
Quality of work	☐	☐	☐	☐	☐
Drawing:					
Holds crayon using tripod (3 fingers)	☐	☐	☐	☐	☐
Has an idea for the drawing (goal)	☐	☐	☐	☐	☐
Two-fold symmetry	☐	☐	☐	☐	☐
Horizontal repetitions (mountains)	☐	☐	☐	☐	☐
Sky and Earth (above – below)	☐	☐	☐	☐	☐
People and houses rest on earth	☐	☐	☐	☐	☐
There is three-folding in figures:					
Person: Head/Torso/Limbs	☐	☐	☐	☐	☐
House: Base/Triangle Roof/Chimney	☐	☐	☐	☐	☐
Tree: Trunk/Leaves/Apples	☐	☐	☐	☐	☐
Draws with detail	☐	☐	☐	☐	☐
Painting:					
Begins to mix colors	☐	☐	☐	☐	☐
Develops designs in paint	☐	☐	☐	☐	☐
Two-fold symmetry	☐	☐	☐	☐	☐

Category	Immature	Progressing	Mature	Concern	N/A
Beeswax:					
Can warm the beeswax easily	☐	☐	☐	☐	☐
Can sculpt forms inspired by story	☐	☐	☐	☐	☐
Circle:					
Enters into activity willingly	☐	☐	☐	☐	☐
Participates in activity	☐	☐	☐	☐	☐
Imitates the gesture of the teacher	☐	☐	☐	☐	☐
Moves with the teacher	☐	☐	☐	☐	☐
Moves with the class	☐	☐	☐	☐	☐
Speaks the verses with the teacher	☐	☐	☐	☐	☐
Sings the songs with the teacher	☐	☐	☐	☐	☐
Internalizes circle	☐	☐	☐	☐	☐
Snack:					
Enters into the activity willingly	☐	☐	☐	☐	☐
Participates in activity	☐	☐	☐	☐	☐
Can pour from pitcher to cup	☐	☐	☐	☐	☐
Can carry cup without spilling	☐	☐	☐	☐	☐
Can eat without making a mess	☐	☐	☐	☐	☐
Can clean up willingly	☐	☐	☐	☐	☐
Story:					
Enters into the activity willingly	☐	☐	☐	☐	☐

Category	Immature	Progressing	Mature	Concern	N/A
Listens to the story attentively	☐	☐	☐	☐	☐
Is able to sit quietly and focus	☐	☐	☐	☐	☐
Internalizes story	☐	☐	☐	☐	☐
Outdoor play:					
Can get ready independently	☐	☐	☐	☐	☐
Can line up with a partner	☐	☐	☐	☐	☐
Can help teacher with equipment	☐	☐	☐	☐	☐
Is responsible with equipment	☐	☐	☐	☐	☐
Can respond to directions	☐	☐	☐	☐	☐
Can react appropriately to discipline	☐	☐	☐	☐	☐
Can resolve conflicts verbally	☐	☐	☐	☐	☐
Transitions:					
Makes transitions easily	☐	☐	☐	☐	☐
Is flexible	☐	☐	☐	☐	☐
Accepts changes	☐	☐	☐	☐	☐
Can wait patiently	☐	☐	☐	☐	☐
Reacts well to new experience	☐	☐	☐	☐	☐
Thinks before doing	☐	☐	☐	☐	☐
Can listen to the teacher	☐	☐	☐	☐	☐
Can move with the group	☐	☐	☐	☐	☐

Kindergarten Assessment Checklist

Name of Child: _____ Date of Birth: _____

Classroom Teacher: _____

Date of assessment: _____

Teacher leading the assessment: _____

Teacher observing the assessment: _____

Physical	Yes	No	Not Progressing
Head-to-body ratio 1:6	☐	☐	☐
Three-folding of body (head/trunk/limbs)	☐	☐	☐
Three-folding of face	☐	☐	☐
Gaze direct eye to eye	☐	☐	☐
Touch top of ear w/arm over head	☐	☐	☐
Neck incision	☐	☐	☐
Waist incision	☐	☐	☐
Limb lengthening	☐	☐	
Visible joints (knuckles and knee caps)	☐	☐	☐
Visible musculature	☐	☐	☐
Arch in foot	☐	☐	☐
S curve in back	☐	☐	☐
Second dentition	☐	☐	☐
Other observations:			

Gross Motor:	Cross lateral	Rhythmic	Coordinated	Other
Walking	☐	☐	☐	☐
Running	☐	☐	☐	☐
Galloping	☐	☐	☐	☐
Slide/Glide	☐	☐	☐	☐
Skipping	☐	☐	☐	☐
Jumping	☐	☐	☐	☐
Hopping (2)	☐	☐	☐	☐

Gross Motor:	Cross lateral	Rhythmic	Coordinated	Other
Hopping (1)	☐	☐	☐	☐
Crawling	☐	☐	☐	☐
Stairs	☐	☐	☐	☐
Catching Ball	☐	☐	☐	☐
Throwing Ball	☐	☐	☐	☐

Other observations:

Origin of Movement

Foot Choice (dominance):   ☐ right   ☐ left   ☐ alternate

Balance Check

1 foot, eyes open	☐ yes	☐ no	☐ other
2 feet, eyes closed	☐ yes	☐ no	☐ other
1 foot, eyes closed	☐ yes	☐ no	☐ other
2 feet, arms crossed, eyes closed	☐ yes	☐ no	☐ other
1 foot, arms crossed, eyes open, speak	☐ yes	☐ no	☐ other
1 foot, arms crossed, eyes closed, speak	☐ successful		☐ struggles
Beam walk	☐ successful		☐ struggles
Sideways, look at feet	☐ successful		☐ struggles
Sideways, do not look at feet, speak	☐ successful		☐ struggles
Forward, heel to toe, may look at feet	☐ successful		☐ struggles
Forward, heel to toe, look straight ahead	☐ successful		☐ struggles
Forward, toe to heel, look straight ahead, speak	☐ successful		☐ struggles

Other observations:

Reflexes

STNR

Hip movement	☐ yes	☐ no	☐ other
Bending of arms	☐ yes	☐ no	☐ other
Leg extension	☐ yes	☐ no	☐ other

Other observations:

Galant

Bend back toward movement	☐ yes	☐ no	☐ other
Hip movement	☐ yes	☐ no	☐ other

ATNR

Opposite arm bend	☐ yes	☐ no	☐ other
Movement in arm	☐ yes	☐ no	☐ other

Other observations:

TLR

Maintain balance	☐ yes	☐ no	☐ other
Roll over L or R	☐ yes	☐ no	☐ other
Head stay curled	☐ yes	☐ no	☐ other

Other observations:

Landau

Sustain raised head	☐ yes	☐ no	☐ other
Sustain raised trunk	☐ yes	☐ no	☐ other
Sustain raised legs	☐ yes	☐ no	☐ other
Sustain raised arms	☐ yes	☐ no	☐ other

Other observations:

Midlines

Horizontal (pick-up gems)	☐ yes	☐ no	☐ other
Vertical (bean bag toss)	☐ yes	☐ no	☐ other

Other Observations:

Body Geography

Mirrored movement

Head both hands	☐ yes	☐ no	☐ other
Shoulders both hands	☐ yes	☐ no	☐ other
Right hand on right hip	☐ yes	☐ no	☐ other
Left hand left knee	☐ yes	☐ no	☐ other
Knees both hands	☐ yes	☐ no	☐ other
Toes both hands	☐ yes	☐ no	☐ other

Directed movement

Right hand on right ear	☐ yes	☐ no	☐ other
Right hand left shoulder	☐ yes	☐ no	☐ other
Left hand on right knee	☐ yes	☐ no	☐ other
Knees both hands	☐ yes	☐ no	☐ other
Toes both hands	☐ yes	☐ no	☐ other

Other observations:

Look for confusion or hesitation

Pick up stones	☐ successful	☐ hesitation	☐ confusion
Bean bag toss	☐ successful	☐ hesitation	☐ confusion
Form drawing journey	☐ successful	☐ hesitation	☐ confusion

Auditory Memory

First	☐ yes	☐ no
Second	☐ yes	☐ no
Third	☐ yes	☐ no

Other observations:

Dominance	Hand		Ear	
First shell	☐ Right	☐ Left	☐ Right	☐ Left
Second shell	☐ Right	☐ Left	☐ Right	☐ Left
Third shell	☐ Right	☐ Left	☐ Right	☐ Left

Other observations:

Eyes - Dominance	Hand		Eye	
First kaleidoscope	☐ Right	☐ Left	☐ Right	☐ Left
Second kaleidoscope	☐ Right	☐ Left	☐ Right	☐ Left
Third kaleidoscope	☐ Right	☐ Left	☐ Right	☐ Left
Eyes – Hole in paper	☐ Right	☐ Left	☐ Right	☐ Left

Other observations:

Eyes - Convergence

Do eyes track together?	☐ yes	☐ no
Circle	☐ yes	☐ no
Back and forth	☐ yes	☐ no
Up and down	☐ yes	☐ no
At an angle	☐ yes	☐ no

Other observations:

Double image: How many inches from nose? _____

Attach the following drawing samples:
☐ Journey in form drawing
☐ Eye color affinity (blue moon/red sun)
☐ Cross test
☐ PHT

Kindergarten Assessment Story

Once upon a time a little boy/girl lived in a village in a far away land. This little boy/girl had a wonderful life in the village. Above all the best part of his/her life was listening to stories told by a woman that everyone in the village called Grandmother. She told many stories, but the one the little boy/girl loved the most was a tale about a faraway kingdom where there lived a king who loved everyone. Finding this kingdom was extremely difficult, but once you found it, you would be happier there than you could ever imagine.

Above all, the little boy/girl yearned to find this kingdom and one day when he/she was almost seven years old, he/she asked Grandmother, "How can I find this kingdom?"

Grandmother replied, "The way is extremely difficult, but I think you are almost ready to begin. Let's see if you are. The king of the kingdom will expect you to salute him in a certain way. I will show you now. (Hand over head and touches ear) You may try to salute the same way. Don't forget this salute. The king will also ask you to shake hands, so let's practice. Yes, I think you are ready for the journey and I can help you prepare for it." So Grandmother and the little boy/girl began to practice for the journey.

"First," said Grandmother, "the way to the kingdom is long and we must become strong and skillful."Come. Follow me. We will start by walking. I will place two stones on the ground, and we will walk in a circle using these stones as guides. Let us make three circles. Follow me.

"Now we will run, but when we run in the forest, we must be able to stop quickly if we see an animal. So this time we will start where one stone is and run to the other stone. You must run to the second stone and not go past it. Let's try this three times.

"Now let's imagine we see wild horses along the way. Let's follow them galloping in a circle around the stones three rounds.

"Sometimes we will find narrow ledges to walk on, especially when we climb the mountain to the kingdom, so this time we will slide sideways between the two stones. Come, follow me. We will go back and forth three times.

"Now, sometimes you will be in a meadow and you can make better time if you skip through the meadow, but let us skip in the same way we walked — in a circle around the two stones. Let's skip around the stones three times.

"Then there are times we will need to jump high to get an apple from the branches of a tree. Let's jump — one, two, and three."

"Then sometimes we will need to jump over puddles. These three lines represent puddles. Let's jump over them. We will jump back and forth three times.

"Sometimes we will need to hop on one foot when the path is really narrow. Can you hop back and forth on one foot three times?

"Sometimes you will need to crawl through long tunnels, some of them as long as three times this room. Let's crawl through the tunnel by going in a circle around the two stones three times.

"Along the way you may find many staircases. We shall practice going up and down the stairs three times.

"When you arrive at the castle of the kingdom, you will find that the king has a son. The young prince loves to play catch. We will practice so you will be ready to play catch with the prince. (Play catch.)

"When you are traveling, you will sometimes do many things that you might not do here in our village. You must be able to stay very quiet, sometimes standing on one foot and closing your eyes to hear better in the forest. You must be very strong to do this. Let's practice different ways of standing quiet — so quiet that a mouse wouldn't even notice you.

"Your eyes must be able to follow a butterfly, even in the dark. Let's practice watching this little butterfly, but you must be down on the ground for the butterfly to come near you. Let me show you. (Balance check)

"You may lie down on your back and rest your eyes. Can you stretch your feet and head at the same time and wiggle your toes at your smile? Now curl up like a caterpillar and see how long you can stay this way. (STNR/ATNR: Spinal Galant Check)

"The forest is enchanted and the great eagles will sometimes carry you over the darkest part of the forest, but you must stretch out your arms and legs and hold you head high just like a great eagle to help them carry you. Let's practice for a long flight over the forest. (TNR/TLR)

"Now, sometimes you will find hints that you are going the right way as you travel to the kingdom. One hint is that you will find little gemstones in the grass. These are very special stones and if you do not treat them gently they will turn into dust. It is important that you gather what you find and carry the stones to the king as a gift. Here is a little pouch for the stones. Pick up stones one by one from the floor and put them gently into your pouch.

"When you arrive at the castle, the guard at the gate will want to know that you are honest and of good will. He will ask you to prove that you mean no harm and can follow directions. I will pretend to be the guard and you must do exactly what I do. (Mirrored Movement) Now listen carefully to my words and follow my directions. (Directed Movement) Finally, he will ask you to show him how clever you are with you hands, because it is important that you are clever and capable when you meet the king. (Bean bag toss)

"Now we have practiced traveling for such a long time, let's sit down and have a little rest. You will need a map to find you way back to the village. Here is a piece of paper and crayons. (The paper will have the corresponding forms for the child to imitate already drawn.) Let's make a map of our travels. First we walked over fields where the flowers were growing. You may use a green crayon and draw the flowers like this. First follow with your finger, now draw it by yourself.

"Then we traveled through the forest where we saw many trees that had large roots. You may use a brown crayon and draw the roots like this. First, follow with your finger, now draw it by yourself.

"Then we hopped over puddles. You may use an orange crayon and draw how we hopped like this. First follow with your finger, now draw it by yourself.

"Then we climbed many mountains. You may use an orange crayon and draw the mountains like this. First follow with your finger, now draw it by yourself.

"We crossed a stream. You may use a blue crayon and draw the water to look like this. First watch me, then follow with your finger, now draw it by yourself.

"The stream will take us to the ocean. You may use a purple crayon and draw the waves to look like this. First follow with your finger, now draw it by yourself.

"After a long time we see the castle. You may use the golden yellow crayon and draw the top of the castle to look like this First follow with your finger, now draw it by yourself.

"On the top of the castle there is a red flag with a golden star. You may draw the flag now. You may put your name on the bottom of your picture.

"You must have very quick eyes and sensitive ears while you are traveling to the kingdom. Let's practice listening. Here are three shells that I found on the beach. I've heard that the sound of the ocean is in every shell. Pick up each one and tell me if you can hear the ocean. (Auditory Memory)

"Now here are three telescopes. Pick up each one, one at a time and look through it. Here is a little butterfly. Follow it with your eyes.

"Now I have put a little hole in this piece of paper, hold it up to your eye and tell me what you see through the hole. (Vision)

"When you reach the castle the guard at the gate will want to know if you have coins from every country in the world. Here are some coins. Make certain they are real coins. Turn each one over carefully. Now that you are certain they are real coins from every country in the world, pick each one up and put it carefully into this little box to give to the king.

"You will always need to look to the sun and the moon to find your way on your journey. On this piece of paper draw a blue moon and a red sun. Now choose a crayon and draw a line down the center of the paper. In one of the spaces draw an x anywhere on the paper. (Dominance Form)

"You have done very well and practiced hard. You are almost ready to take the journey to the castle. But first I must know that you will always remember where you come from. I am going to ask you to draw a picture, but first we must practice a few more things. (Clapping and jumping exercise)

"Now sit down and draw a picture of a person, a house and a tree on this piece of paper. (Person House Tree Picture)

"Finally, do you remember how you must salute the king? Show me now."

Ripeness for Elementary School

The question which presents itself when it comes to first grade readiness is: "Why can't we simply change the acceptance age for first grade to seven after Easter?" This readiness milestone is clearly and concisely laid out by Rudolf Steiner and many educators, and studies support a later age.

As Waldorf teachers we have a responsibility to understand the pictures given to us by Steiner in *The Foundation of Human Development* regarding the evolutionary development of the human being. The integrating of the four bodies of man, the relationships between our spirit and our physical aspects, and the constant recapitulation we undergo as we obtain new capacities which connect us to evolutionary human history.

So why can't we simply honor this seven-year milestone? Money is the problem. There is a fear that if we do not follow the same rules that are followed in public education, we will lose enrollment. These early enrollments are doing damage and yet we do not stand up for what we know to be true—that is, that the human being is simply not ready for elementary school until he has turned seven years old. We use excuses to justify our failure to not comply, such as parental pressure (money), precociousness (competition), and karma. Karma is possibly the worst of reasons since the child is probably with the children he is meant to be with, but they are all entering school together too early.

There is one other problem: The kindergarten is not prepared to offer a curriculum which will meet the needs of the developing human being past the age of six. Many teachers fight to hold back children whom they sense are not ready, and then in the end are compelled to move them on because they cannot continue to meet their needs.

What would meet the child who is not yet ready for elementary school but cannot be met in the kindergarten? A gardening program or a farming program, age-appropriate handwork and craft projects, and cooking would sufficiently help the children integrate their bodies and be ready for learning in the classroom. A transitional kindergarten is really what is needed for children who are six. I have often thought that if the three-year-old is not ready for a mixed-age kindergarten, then the polarity on the older end of the kindergarten probably needs something more or different as well.

Often the children who are not ready to move on in September are children born in the summer. These children, often boys, show signs of readiness, but the signs are inconsistent. Many summer children could be ready to move midyear. It is important to consider the summer child because often they do not need an extra year of kindergarten but they do need time. A study done by James K. Uphoff and June E. Gilmore in the Midwest showed that summer children were more likely to read later, to show signs of behavior problems, to be placed in special education categories, and to repeat grades. They even recorded a higher number of teenage suicides among summer-born children. (Uphoff, Gilmore, and Huber, 1986)

What Do We Need to Know at This Transition?

We need to know that children have the capacity to meet the expectations in the elementary school successfully. Children need to be ready for the authority of the teacher in first grade, to meet the teacher's gaze, shake the teacher's hand and follow the teacher's lead. Children need to be fully incorporated into their bodies by first grade. They must have a three-folding in all parts of their bodies so they can sit in an upright posture at a desk and write and draw and manage the rhythmical movement in the curriculum. They must be capable of body-based learning and have fine motor skills to learn to knit and hold a pencil. Children also need to have the social skills to move and work with their classmates and the consciousness to focus beyond their desk.

Some children will rise to first grade before they are ready and some children will have hindrances to overcome. Even when such children are admitted to first grade, there should be a picture that they have the maturity to work with the hindrance and still be successful as an elementary school student. This picture can be perceived though a long term observation process in the kindergarten.

The Importance of Record Keeping

The process for observation and assessment that needs to happen during the early childhood years is such that it informs the teacher of the child's development and progress. The teachers, through informed observation, can conference more effectively, write reports more effectively and interact with colleagues more effectively to support the healthy development of the children who are in their care. By developing conference logs, check lists and assessments, a teacher can follow the biography of an individual child and determine the health of the classroom when a child is in need of extra care. Early childhood is a time of constant movement and change. It is important not to set too much in stone, but it is also important to have a recorded picture of the child's early development, something more than the memory of the teacher or the parent. (See an example of a parent-friendly "Final Kindergarten Report" at the end of this section.) The experience the child has when introduced to the world is a vital part of the human biography and early childhood is the beginning chapter of the child's life.

A process for observation and assessment is also an important and supportive baseline for research that substantiates the work being done in Waldorf schools. This work is important and vital to the development of human beings and the social direction and development of the world. Waldorf schools need to present a true picture of the developing human being and effectively prove how the curriculum meets that picture. What better way to do this than through recorded observation and assessment?

Final Kindergarten Report

Name of Child: _____

Date of Birth: _____

Dominance: Right ☐   Left ☐   Not Established ☐

Checklist	Yes	No
Touch top of ear	☐	☐
Waist and neck incisions	☐	☐
Visible joints	☐	☐
Three-folding of limbs	☐	☐
Arch in foot	☐	☐
Individualized facial features	☐	☐
Second dentition	☐	☐
Walk a beam	☐	☐
Catch a ball	☐	☐
Throw a ball	☐	☐
Hop on either foot	☐	☐
Walk in cross pattern	☐	☐
Climb stairs alternating feet	☐	☐
Tie shoes/knots or bows	☐	☐
Button and zip jacket	☐	☐
Able to sew	☐	☐
Able to finger knit	☐	☐
Enjoys telling jokes	☐	☐
Sense of privacy	☐	☐

Comments:

Teacher:_____   Date:_____

ACKNOWLEDGEMENTS

This book is dedicated to Paolo Marino who lit the fire of enthusiasm within my soul for this path in my teaching, and to all of the children I have had the privilege to spend time with in the classroom. You are my teachers far more than I was a teacher to you.

I also dedicate it to my family: my husband Michael, my daughter Anna and my son Samuel. Without your love and support I would never have found the courage to continue teaching.

As in all endeavors there are many people to thank. I would like to thank my editor, David Mitchell, who gathered my words and formed them into this beautiful book.

I am particularly grateful to Dee Joy Coulter who steadfastly stood by my side as I wrote. Dee was always present supporting my work, encouraging me to move forward, and protecting my process. I am also exceedingly grateful to Stevie Ross who was a trustworthy first reader of my manuscript. I could not hope for a greater friend or a more supportive colleague.

Finally, I want to express my gratitude to Rudolf Steiner who opened the way to truth, beauty and goodness in education and developed a curriculum that recognizes individual human freedom.

APPENDIX

Andersen, R.A., Essick, G.K., and Siegel, R.M. (1985). Encoding of spatial location by posterior parietal neurons. *Science*, 230, 456–458. This study explores the receptivity of the visual field, concluding that visual neurons are the most receptive when the visual context is fixed on center.

Brodfuehrer, P.D. and Friesen, W.O. (1986). From stimulation to undulation: a neuronal pathway for the control of swimming in the Leech. *Science*, 234, 1002–1004. This is a study of how movement is initiated, concluding that movement is a reaction to a process of detection on the cellular level no matter what the name of the cell.

Cohen, B., Rapan, T. and Waespe, W. (1985). Dynamic modification of the vestibulo-ocular reflex by the nodulus and uvula. *Science*. 228, 199–202.

Koshland, D.E, Goldbeter, A. and Stock, J.B. (1982). Amplification and adaptation in regulatory and sensory systems. *Science*, 217, 220–225. This is a study of the effect of environment on living organisms, concluding that there is not a different cell for regulation and sensation and amplification and that adaptation occurs because of a response to the environment.

Poggion, T. and Koch, C. (1987). Synapses that compute motion. *Scientific American*, 256(5), 46–52. This is a study of how nerve cells in the eye process the information they receive from the environment, concluding that something in the space between cells detects motion which is what initiates visual experience, and determines our visual understanding, and puts our perception of what we 'see' in context. There is an optimal visual field; vision depends on movement, which is detected not by the cell but between cells. We respond to sensations by tuning in and adapting to what is in the environment, there is a relationship to movement, and intentional movement is a reaction to detection of environmental change on a cellular level.

Raloff, J. (1988) Lead effects show in child's balance. *Science News*, 135(4), 54.

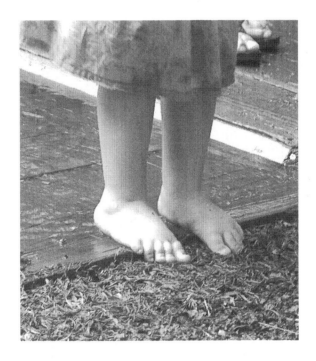

REFERENCES

Almon, J. (1988). Further considerations about kindergarten readiness. *Waldorf Kindergarten Newsletter*, 2–5.

Apgar, V. (July-Aug, 1953). A proposal for a new method of evaluation of the newborn infant, current researches in anesthesia and analgesia. *Neonatology on the Web*. Retrieved July 25, 2008 from, http://www.neonatology.org.

Ayres, A.J. (2000). *Sensory Integration and the Child*. Los Angeles: Western Psychological Services.

Coulter, D.J. (1999). *An Immature Movement Response which Interferes with Reading; The Vertical Midline Barrier, Learning Difficulties, A Guide for Teachers*. Willby, M.E. (Ed.). Fair Oaks, CA: Rudolf Steiner College Press.

Goddard, S. (2002). *Reflexes, Learning and Behavior, A Window into the Child's Mind*. Eugene, OR: Fern Ridge Press.

Gootman, E. (August 26, 2008). "A plan to test the city's youngest pupils." *New York Times, Education Section*.

König, K. (2009). *On Reading & Writing*. AWSNA Publications, Electronics Books, Number 2.

Lievegoed, B. (1985). *Phases of Childhood*. Great Barrington, MA: Anthroposophic Press.

McAllen, A.E. (2004). *Sleep*. Fair Oaks, CA: Rudolf Steiner College Press.

Pierangelo, R. & Giuliani, G. (1998). *Special Educator's Complete*

Guide to 109 Diagnostic Tests. West Nyack, NY: The Center for Applied Research in Education.

Ratey, J.J. (2002). *A User's Guide to the Brain.* New York: Vintage Books.

Soesman, A. (2000). *Our Twelve Senses: Wellsprings of the Soul.* Gloucestershire, UK: Hawthorn Press.

Steiner, R. (1998). *Education for Special Needs, The Curative Education Course.* London: Rudolf Steiner Press.

_____. (1996a). *The Foundations of Human Experience.* Great Barrington, MA: Anthroposophic Press.

_____. (1994). *How to Know Higher Worlds.* Great Barrington, MA: Anthroposophic Press.

_____. (1995). *Self-Education in the Light of Spiritual Science.* Chestnut Ridge, NY: Mercury Press.

_____. (1906). *The Threefold Social Order and Educational Freedom.* GA 24, Rudolf Steiner Archive. Retrieved, April 2, 2007, http//www.rsarchive.org.

_____. (1994). *Theosophy.* Great Barrington, MA: Anthroposophic Press.

Swain, J. (2008). "Emmi Pickler's trust in the wise infant, a warm and gentle welcome: nurturing children from birth to age three. Spring Valley," NY: WECAN.

Uphoff, J,K., Gilmore, J.E. & Huber, R. (1986). *Summer Children Ready or Not for School.* Hollywood, FL: J&J Publishing Company.

Zajonc, A. (2009). *Meditation as Contemplative Inquiry.* Great Barrington, MA: Lindisfarne Books.

BIBLIOGRAPHY

Aeppli, W. (1998). *The Care and Development of the Human Senses.* East Sussex, UK: Steiner Schools Fellowship Publications.

Ayres, A.J. (2000). *Sensory Integration and the Child.* Los Angeles: Western Psychological Services.

Baldwin, R. (1989). *You Are Your Child's First Teacher.* San Francisco: Celestial Arts.

Blythe, S. G. (2004). *The Well Balanced Child.* Gloucestershire, UK: Hawthorn Press.

Brazelton, T.B. and Greenspan, S.I. (2000). *The Irreducible Deeds of Children.* Cambridge, MA: Perseus Publishing.

Brearley, M. (Ed.) (1975). *The Teaching of Young Children, Some Applications of Piaget's Learning Theory.* New York: Schoken Books.

Bristol, E. (1998). *Practicalities of the Meditative Path.* Great Barrington, MA: Anthroposophical Society.

Dewey, J. (1974). *John Dewey on Education, Selected Writings.* Chicago: The University of Chicago Press.

Dewey, J. (1990). *The School and Society and the Child and the Curriculum.* Chicago: The University of Chicago Press.

Eikenboom, J. (2007). *Foundations of the Extra Lesson.* Fair Oaks, CA: Rudolf Steiner College Press.

Elkind, D. (1976). *Child Development and Education.* New York: Oxford University Press.

_____. (1987). *Miseducation: Preschoolers at Risk*. New York: Alfred A. Knopf.

Erickson, Erik H. (1985). *Childhood and Society*. New York: W.W. Norton and Company.

Goddard, S. (2002). *Reflexes, Learning and Behavior, a Window into the Child's Mind*. Eugene, OR: Fern Ridge Press.

Glas, N. (1983). *Conception, Birth and Early Childhood*. Great Barrington, MA: Anthroposophic Press.

Glöckler, M. (2000). *A Healing Education*. Fair Oaks, CA: Rudolf Steiner College Press.

_____. (2002). *Education as Preventive Medicine, A Salutogenic Approach*. Fair Oaks, CA: Rudolf Steiner College Press.

Greenspan, S. and Greenspan, N.T. (1989). *First Feelings*. New York: Penguin Books.

Greenspan, S.I. (1997). *The Growth of the Mind and the Endangered Origins of Intelligence*. Reading, MA: Addison-Wesley Publishing Company, Inc.

Groh, I. and Ruef, M. (2002). *Education and Teaching as Preventative Medicine*. Dornach: Medical Section at the Goetheanum.

Healy, J.M. (2001). *Your Child's Growing Mind*. New York: Broadway Books.

_____. (1990). *Endangered Minds*. New York: Simon & Schuster.

_____. (1998). *Failure to Connect*. New York: Simon & Schuster.

Hunter, M. (1995). *Improved Instruction*. Thousand Oaks, CA: Corwin Press, Inc.

Jaffke, F. (2000). *Toy Making with Children*. Edinburgh: Floris Books.

_____. (2000). *Work and Play in Early Childhood*. Great Barrington, MA: Anthroposophic Press.

Jenkinson, S. (2004). *The Genius of Play: Celebrating the Spirit of Childhood*. Gloucestershire, UK: Hawthorn Press.

Köhler, H. (2003). *Difficult Children: There Is no Such Thing*. Fair Oaks, CA: AWSNA Publications.

_____. (2001). *Working with Anxious, Nervous, and Depressed Children*. Fair Oaks, CA: AWSNA Publications.

König, K. (1989). *Being Human*. Great Barrington, MA: Anthroposophic Press.

_____. (1994). *Eternal Childhood*. Camphill, PA: Camphill Books.

_____. (1969). *The First Three Years of the Child*. Great Barrington, MA: Anthroposophic Press.

_____. (2002). *On Reading and Writing*. Camphill, PA: Camphill Books.

Kuhlewind, G. (2008). *The Light of the 'I.'* (Ed. Bamford, C.). Great Barrington, MA: Lindisfarne Press.

Levine, M. (2002). *A Mind at a Time*. New York: Simon & Schuster.

_____. (2003). *The Myth of Laziness*. New York: Simon & Schuster Paperbacks.

_____. (2005). *Ready or Not, Here Life Comes*. New York: Simon & Schuster.

Lievegoed, B. (1985). *Phases of Childhood*. Great Barrington, MA: Floris Books, Anthroposophic Press.

Lowndes, F. (2001). *Enlivening the Charkra of the Heart.* Vancouver, BC: Sophia Books.

McAllen, A.E. (2004). *The Extra Lesson.* Fair Oaks, CA: Rudolf Steiner College Press.

_____. (2004). *Reading Children's Drawings, The Person, House and Tree Motifs.* Fair Oaks, CA: Rudolf Steiner College Press.

_____. (2004). *Sleep.* Fair Oaks, CA: Rudolf Steiner College Press.

Mitchell, D.S. (2002). *Developmental Insights.* AWSNA Curriculum Series.

Oldfield, L. (2001). *Free to Learn.* Gloucestershire, UK: Hawthorn Press.

Oresti, M.J. & Ross, R. *Care Group Manual, a Practical Approach.* Association for a Healing Education.

Piaget, J. (1962). *Play, Dreams and Imitation in Childhood.* New York: W.W. Norton & Company.

Piaget, J. and Inhelder, B. (1969). *The Psychology of the Child.* New York: Basic Books Inc. Publishers.

Pierangelo, R. and Giuliani, G. (1998). *Special Educator's Complete Guide to 109 Diagnostic Tests.* West Nyack, NY: The Center for Applied Research in Education.

Ratey, J.J. (2002). *A User's Guide to the Brain.* New York: Vintage Books.

Rawson, M. and Rose, M. (2002). *Ready to Learn: From Birth to School Readiness.* Gloucestershire, UK: Hawthorn Press.

Scharff, P.W. (1995). *Threefolding.* Chestnut Ridge, NY: Mercury Press.

Schoorel, E. (2004). *The First Seven Years: Physiology of Childhood.* Fair Oaks, CA: Rudolf Steiner College Press.

Selg, P. (2008). *The Therapeutic Eye.* London: Steiner Books.

Singer, D.G. and Revenson, T.A. (1978). *A Piaget Primer: How a Child Thinks.* New York: New American Library.

Smit, J. (1992). *The Child, the Teachers and the Community.* Chestnut Ridge, NY: Mercury Press.

_____. (1992). *Lighting Fires: Deepening Education through Meditation.* Gloucestershire, UK: Hawthorn Press.

Soesman, A. (2000). *Our Twelve Senses: Wellsprings of the Soul.* Gloucestershire, UK: Hawthorn Press.

Spock, M. (1983). *Group Moral Artistry I: Reflections on Community Building.* Spring Valley, NY: St. George Publications.

_____. (1983). *Group Moral Artistry II: the Art of Goethean Conversation.* Spring Valley, NY: St. George Publications.

Steiner, R. (1984). *Art as Seen in the Light of Mystery Wisdom.* London: Rudolf Steiner Press.

_____. (1982). *Balance in Teaching.* Chestnut Ridge, NY: Mercury Press.

_____. (1996). *The Child's Changing Consciousness.* Great Barrington, MA: Anthroposophic Press.

_____. (1988). *Conferences with the Teachers of the Waldorf School in Stuttgart 1922-23,* Volume Three, conference of Tuesday, February 6, 1923. Essex, UK: Steiner Schools Fellowship Publications.

_____. (1980). *Course for Young Doctors, Bridge Lectures.* Chestnut Ridge, NY: Mercury Press.

_____. (1983). *Discussions with Teachers*. London: Rudolf Steiner Press.

_____. (1996). *The Education of the Child*. Great Barrington, MA: Anthroposophic Press.

_____. (1998). *Education for Special Needs, the Curative Education Course*. London: Rudolf Steiner Press.

_____. (1996). *The Foundations of Human Experience*. Great Barrington, MA: Anthroposophic Press.

_____. (1981). *The Four Sacrifices of Christ*. Great Barrington, MA: Anthroposophic Press.

_____. (1999). *Fundamentals of Therapy*. Chestnut Ridge, NY: Mercury Press.

_____. (1973). *The Gospel of St. John*. Great Barrington, MA: The Anthroposophic Press.

_____. (1988). *The Gospel of St. Luke*. London: Rudolf Steiner Press.

_____. (1994). *How to Know Higher Worlds*. Great Barrington, MA: Anthroposophic Press.

_____. (1999). *Introducing Anthroposophical Medicine Volume 1*. Great Barrington, MA: Anthroposophic Press.

_____. (1995). *Intuitive Thinking as a Spiritual Path*. Great Barrington, MA: Anthroposophic Press.

_____. (1987). *The Invisible Man within Us – the Pathology Underlying Therapy*. Chestnut Ridge, NY: Mercury Press.

_____. (1988). *Kingdom of Childhood*. Great Barrington, MA: Anthroposophic Press.

_____. (1998). *Love and Its Meaning in the World*. Great Barrington, MA: Anthroposophic Press.

_____. (1981). *Man as a Being of Sense and Perception*. North Vancouver, BC: Steiner Book Centre, Inc.

_____. (1987). *Pastoral Medicine*. Great Barrington, MA: Anthroposophic Press.

_____. (1988). *Practical Advice to Teachers*. London: Rudolf Steiner Press.

_____. (1961). *Pre-earthly Deeds of Christ*. North Vancouver, BC: Steiner Book Centre, Inc.

_____. (1999). *A Psychology of Body, Soul and Spirit*. Great Barrington, MA: Anthroposophic Press.

_____. (1995). *Self-Education in the Light of Spiritual Science*. Chestnut Ridge, NY: Mercury Press.

_____. (1986). *Soul Economy and Waldorf Education*. Great Barrington, MA: Anthroposophic Press.

_____. (1995). *The Spiritual Foundation of Morality*. Great Barrington, MA: Anthroposophic Press.

_____. (1994). *Theosophy*. Great Barrington, MA: Anthroposophic Press.

_____. (1975). *Understanding Young Children*, extracts from lectures for kindergarten teachers. Stuttgart: International Association of Waldorf Kindergartens. London: Rudolf Steiner Press.

_____. (1979). *The World of the Senses and the World of the Spirit*. Great Barrington, MA: Anthroposophic Press.

Strauss, M. (2007). *Understanding Children's Drawings*. London: Rudolf Steiner Press.

Tautz, J. (1990). *The Meditative Life of the Teacher*. Chestnut Ridge, NY: Mercury Press.

Uphoff, J.K., Gilmore, J.E. & Huber, R. (1986). *Summer Children Ready or Not for School*. Hollywood, FL: J&J Publishing Co.

Von Heydebrand, C. (1995). *Childhood: A Study of the Growing Child*. Great Barrington, MA: Anthroposophic Press.

Vygotsky, L.S. (1978). *Mind in Society: the Development of Higher Psychological Processes*. Cambridge, MA: Harvard University Press.

Willby, M. (Ed.). (1999). *Learning Difficulties: A Guide for Teachers*. Fair Oaks, CA: Rudolf Steiner College Press.

Zajonc, A. (2009). *Meditation as Contemplative Inquiry*. Great Barrington, MA: Lindisfarne Books.

Lectures:

Steiner, R. (May 26, 1922). *The Human Heart*, Dornach, GA 212.

_____. (February 25, 1911). *The Work of the Ego in Childhood: A Contribution Towards an Understanding of Christ*. Zurich: Translated by Dorothy S. Osmond.

Articles:

Almon, J. (2004). First grade readiness. Howard, S. (Ed.) The developing child: the first seven years. *The Gateways Series Three*. 119–130. Spring Valley, NY: WECAN.

_____. (Winter 1988). Further considerations about kindergarten readiness. *Waldorf Kindergarten Newsletter*, 2–5.

_____. (2004). The vital role of play in childhood, the developing child: the first seven years. *The Gateways Series Three*. 85–94. Spring Valley, NY: WECAN.

Apgar, V. (July-Aug, 1953). A proposal for a new method of evaluation of the newborn infant, current researches in anesthesia and analgesia. *Neonatology on the Web*. Retrieved July 25, 2008, http://www.neonatology.org.

Blakeslee, S. (March 7, 2000). For better learning, researchers endorse "sleep on it" adage. *New York Times*.

Clark, L. and Blanning, N. (April 2003). Strengthening the lower senses. *Association for a Healing Education Newsletter*, 3–4.

Coulter, D.J. (1999). An immature movement response which interferes with reading; the vertical midline barrier, learning difficulties, a guide for teachers. Willby, Mary E. (Ed.) *Learning Difficulties, A Guide for Teachers*. Fair Oaks, CA: Rudolf Steiner College Press, 60–63.

Foster, N. (2004). Some guidelines for first grade readiness, the developing child: the first seven years. *The Gateways Series Three*. 131–136. Spring Valley, NY: WECAN.

Gambardella, A. (2006). Observing the young child. *Gateways*. Issue 51, 32–35.

Ginsburg, K.R. (2007). The importance of play in promoting healthy child development and maintaining strong parent-child bonds. *American Academy of Pediatrics*. Retrieved January, 2007, http://www.aap.org.

Glöckler, M. (2004). The birth of the etheric: transformation of growth forces into thinking forces, the developing child: the first seven years. *The Gateways Series Three*. 111–117. Spring Valley, NY: WECAN.

_____. (2004). Forces of growth and forces of fantasy: understanding the dream consciousness of the young child, the developing child: the first seven years. *The Gateways Series Three*. 73–83. Spring Valley, NY: WECAN.

Gootman, E. (August 26, 2008). A plan to test the city's youngest pupils. *New York Times*, Education Section.

Howard, S. (2006). The essentials of Waldorf early childhood education. *Gateways*. Issue 51, 6–12.

Jacobi, E. (2004). Kindergarten readiness, the developing child: the first seven years. *The Gateways Series Three*. 109–110. Spring Valley, NY: WECAN.

Jaffke, F. (2004). Stages of development in early childhood, the developing child: the first seven years. *The Gateways Series Three*. 7–12. Spring Valley, NY: WECAN.

Meisels, S.J. (January 1987). Uses and abuses of developmental screening and school readiness testing. *Young Children*, 4–6, 68–73.

Moore-Haas, E. (1989). The religion of the young child. *Waldorf Kindergarten Newsletter*, 6–11.

Ogletree, E.J. (1990). School readiness: the developmental view. *Steiner Education*, Vol. 24, No. 2, 23–30.

Patterson, B. (April, 2003). Remedial work in early childhood. *Association for a Healing Education Newsletter*, 5–6.

Royeen, C.B. (1986). The development of a touch scale for measuring tactile defensiveness in children. *The American Journal of Occupational Therapy.* Vol. 40, Number 6, 414–419.

Steiner, R. (1906). *The Threefold Social Order and Educational Freedom, the Three-fold Social Order.* GA 24, Rudolf Steiner Archive. Retrieved April 2, 2007, http://www.rsarchive.

Swain, J. (2008). Emmi Pickler's trust in the wise infant. *The Gateways Series Five,* 19–26. Spring Valley, NY: WECAN.

Weber, S. (2008). Fostering healthy language development in young children: a journey in relationships. *The Gateways Series Five,* 35–40. Spring Valley, NY: WECAN.

Wenner, M. (January 29, 2009). The serious need for play. *Scientific American.* Retrieved February 2, 2009, http://www.sciam.com/article.cfm?id=the-serious-need-for-play&page=2.

Zahlingen, Bronja. (2004). Movement, gesture and language in the life of the young child, the developing child: the first seven years. *The Gateways Series Three,* 43–48. Spring Valley, NY: WECAN.

Other Materials:

Coulter, D.J. (2003). Alternating cycles of development (unpublished class notes).

_____. (1993). Developmental milestones (unpublished class notes).

_____. (2004). Guiding the will development of children (unpublished class notes).

United States Department of Education. (2001). *No Child Left Behind Act,* Retrieved December 2008, http://www.ed.gov/nclb/landing.jhtml.

Printed in Great Britain
by Amazon.co.uk, Ltd.,
Marston Gate.